<One Show Interactive> Advertising's Best
Interactive & New Media

Volume Two

<president>	Bob Barrie
<executive director>	Mary Warlick
<interactive director>	Kevin Swanepoel
<one show interactive volume 2>	
<creative director and cover concept>	Kevin Swanepoel
<editors>	Mary Warlick Kevin Swanepoel
<contributing editor>	Mary Jo Fahey
<CD-ROM programmers>	Ogilvy Interactive South Africa Alan Alston Roger Horrocks Kevin Swanepoel
<production assistants>	Steven O'Connell Dave Chang
<design and layout>	Anne Louise Burns Maria Ruotolo
<publisher & distributor>	Rotovision S.A.
<sales office>	Sheridan House 112-116a Western Road Hove, East Sussex, BN3 1DD United Kingdom
<telephone>	1273-72-7268
<fax>	1273-72-7269
<in association with>	The One Club for Art & Copy 32 East 21st Street New York, NY 10010
<telephone>	212-979-1900
<fax>	212-979-5006
<email>	oneclub@inch.com
<web site>	www.oneclub.com
<copyright © 1999>	As a collection by The One Club for Art & Copy, Inc. All rights reserved. No part of this book or CD ROM may be reproduced in any way by any means whatsoever without express permission in writing from the owners.
<first printing>	ISBN 2-88046-474-9
<production & separation>	Provision, Singapore
<telephone>	65-334-7720
<fax>	65-334-7721
<printing>	Singapore

</frameset>
<noframes>

</pageref>
ii><lhp>

</frameset>
<noframes>

</pageref>
<iii><rhp>

The One Club for Art & Copy, based in New York City, was founded in 1975 and is a non-profit organization designed to maintain the highest standards of creativity in advertising. Its 1,000 members include many of advertising's most respected art directors and copywriters, as well as students of advertising.

As part of its mission to promote high standards of creative excellence, The One Club produces the advertising industry's most prestigious awards program, The One Show. Judged by a panel of the advertising industry's elite creative directors, this annual event acknowledges excellence in art direction and copywriting in a variety of categories, including television, radio, newspapers, magazines, billboards and public service announcements. The coveted One Show "Gold Pencils" are regarded as the zenith of achievement in the advertising world.

The One Club regularly produces a variety of events and programs that encourage aspiring advertising types to hone their craft. These programs include:

• "Gold On Gold" lectures
(award-winning industry professionals discuss the creative process)

• Portfolio reviews

• The One Show College Competition

• Creative workshops

• one–a quarterly publication by and for advertising creatives

• One Club gallery exhibitions

• The One Show annual, the indispensable hardcover reference showcasing the best advertising worldwide.

• One Show Interactive annual, the first book of its kind highlighting the best new media advertising.

In 1995, The One Club established an education department, dedicated to fostering the creative talents of advertising students nationwide. The department administers scholarships to outstanding students in advertising programs at a select number of colleges and advertising schools throughout the country. In 1998, The One Club launched One Show Interactive, the first award show dedicated exclusively to advertising in new media. With the first One Show Interactive awards, The One Club extends its mission of recognizing creative excellence to the new media field.

In addition to producing One Show Interactive, The One Club has supported the new media community through a series of exhibitions focusing on new techniques and highlighting creativity in online advertising. "Web Sites at an Exhibition" in 1997 and "New Media at an Exhibition" in 1998 attracted audiences from both traditional advertising sectors and the new media community.

</pageref>
<iv><lhp>

<kevin swanepoel
interactive director
editor>

One Show Interactive is the first awards program to host an event solely for advertising in new media and not as a sub-category in a larger awards competition. By acknowledging the importance of new technology online, interactive is not overshadowed by more traditional forms of advertising. As an international showcase for new media, the event served as a sounding board where new trends and techniques could be evaluated. It furnished a unique opportunity for creative people to see first-hand what other creative people are working on and developing in the new media industry around the world.

This annual is a compilation of all the pencil and merit award winners. The first section contains comments by the creative teams about the strategy, structure and design of their winning work. With the addition of a new category, Integrated Branding, complete campaigns were judged on the effectiveness of integrating their brand successfully across the different media of interactive, print, television and collateral.

The second One Show Interactive annual also contains a collection of corporate profiles of agencies whose work has been recognized in the competition. A number of agencies and interactive companies have chosen One Show Interactive, Volume II, to showcase outstanding work done for their clients, list key personnel and their design philosophy. This additional feature of One Show Interactive will make it an indispensable reference book for the new media industry.

>

</pageref>
<v><rhp>

<the objective>	To award pencils for new media that really excel in all areas — concept, graphic design, architecture and technology. The primary focus must be on meeting an advertising objective.
<concept>	Relating to the creativity of the idea/ mission behind the interactive advertising and the innovative application of technology toward its end.
<graphic design>	When judging the graphic qualities of the work, all aspects related to visual presentation, such as color, type design and page layout were considered.
<copy>	As in conventional advertising, copy can make or break a great ad. The online and new media industry needs to address the "copy" issue; copy is as crucial to the effectiveness of the work as is the design and technology.
<information architecture>	Each entry was judged on its ease of navigation and the degree to which the work's structure, links and interaction effectively achieves its purpose — did the site, banner or digital piece lead the viewer to the most important aspects of the site? Did it hold the viewer's attention? Would it get the viewer to revisit the site?
<innovation>	It was also very important to acknowledge those designers and programmers who creatively used cutting-edge technology to achieve an advertising or branding objective rather than just to produce really "cool stuff" for technology's sake.

</frameset>
<noframes>

</pageref>
<vi><lhp>

<Chris Briggs>	AGENCY.COM/New York
<Joe Duffy>	Duffy Design/Minneapolis
<Stephen Embleton>	Armadillo Interactive/Durban
<Peter Girardi>	Funny Garbage/New York
<John Grotting>	Sapient/San Francisco
<Joel Hladecek>	Red Sky Interactive/San Francisco
<Wichar Jiempreecha>	Rare Medium/New York
<Craig Kanarick>	Razorfish/New York
<Frank Lantz>	R/GA Interactive/New York
<Jan Ulrik Leth>	Ogilvy Interactive/New York
<Marcus Lynam>	Webfactory/Dublin
<Brian Martin>	Think New Ideas/New York
<Joe McCambley>	Modem Media.Poppe Tyson Interactive/Westport
<Miles McManus>	Oven Digital/New York
<Tom Nicholson>	Nicholson NY/New York
<Dan Olson>	Revolv/Minneapolis
<Dave Parrish>	Martin Interactive/Richmond
<Shirley Rafieetary>	Medius IV/San Francisco
<Andrew Sather>	Sapient/San Francisco
<Bronson Smith>	US Interactive/New York
<Robert Wong>	USWeb/CKS/New York

</frameset>
<noframes>

>

</pageref>
<vii><rhp>

<Joe McCambley>Worldwide Executive Creative Director-Modem Media.Poppe Tyson Interactive

Joe is responsible for the overall creative quality of all of Modem Media.Poppe Tyson's accounts including AT&T, Citibank, Delta Airlines, IBM and John Hancock. Joe joined MM.PT from Thunder House, the interactive division of McCann WorldGroup where he served as president, overseeing all strategic and operational aspects of the business. Previously, Joe was Modem Media.Poppe Tyson's Creative Director from 1994 until 1996. Prior to Modem, he spent several years with Bronner Slosberg Humphrey and Ingalls, Quinn & Johnson Advertising, both in Boston.

Joe is a fourth degree blackbelt in Karate, and an expert marksman. When not creating breakthrough work for Modem clients, Joe enjoys breaking cement blocks.

<Craig M. Kanarick>
Chief Scientist-Razorfish

As Chief Scientist and co-founder of Razorfish, Craig Kanarick creates award-winning solutions for clients and plays a prominent role in the nascent digital communications industry. At Razorfish, Craig leads internal learning, best practices, oversees corporate culture and helps define the science of Digital Change Management. Craig holds a B.A. in philosophy and a B.A.S. in computer science from the University of Pennsylvania and an MS in visual studies from MIT where he studied in the Visible Language Workshop at MIT's Media Lab. Prior to co-founding Razorfish with Jeff Dachis in 1995, Craig worked as a digital media consultant and designer in New York City.

<Robert Wong>Partner and Senior Creative Director-USWeb/CKS

Robert was born Chinese, was Dutch for awhile and now he's a Canadian on his way to becoming an American. Enroute to a Master's of Accounting degree in Toronto, Robert bought a ticket to New York City, and wound up getting a BFA in Communication Design from Parsons School of Design. As Partner and Senior Creative Director at USWeb/CKS, Robert has won numerous awards and has successfully led integrated programs of positioning, branding, corporate identity, design, advertising, direct response and new media for clients as diverse as Audi, IBM, Citibank, Sony, MCI, Clinique and Nabisco.

<Bronson Smith>Executive Creative Director-US Interactive

Bronson Smith's background in traditional advertising includes agency work at Della Femina McNamee WCRS/Pittsburgh, Young & Rubicam/Paris and Avrett Free & Ginsberg in New York. Currently Exectuive Creative Director of US Interactive/New York, Bronson's work has garnered numerous industry awards including a Gold Lion at the Cannes International Advertising Festival and the Best of Show at the London International Advertising Awards. He received the President's Award from the Ad Club in 1996 and has been active as a judge for several interactive award competitions including The One Show Interactive Awards, The British Design & Art Direction Awards, The Andy Awards and the London International Advertising Awards.

<Miles McManus>
Creative Director-Oven Digital

Miles trained as a visual artist and computer programmer and is responsible for Oven Digital's unique design philosophy. As Creative Director, he oversees identity design, information design, and interactive design for all Oven Digital projects. Miles holds degrees in Fine Art from the University of Texas and the School of Visual Arts.

</pageref>
<viii><lhp>

Frank Lantz/Creative Director/
Interaction Design-R/GA Interactive

As a founding member of R/GA-I, Frank has helped to define the
overall goals and strategies of the company over the course of
its evolution. Frank has worked on or overseen the production
of websites, CD-ROMs, and kiosks for clients such as IBM, Intel,
Sothebys.com, Brooklyn Academy of Music, Ticketmaster,
Microsoft and French Connection UK. He is also the co-designer
of the game Gearheads, published by Philips Media, and The
Robot Club, an educational CD-ROM which was released in 1999.
Frank is a regular contributor to I.D. Magazine and received a
BA in Studio Art from the University of Maryland in 1986.

<Peter Girardi>Creative Director-
Funny Garbage

Peter Girardi is a pioneer in
both website design and CD-
ROM production. After
designing and producing Body
Voyage, Maus, Painters
Painting, The Beat Experience,
and People Magazine CD-ROM
titles for Voyager, Peter formed
his own digital design firm,
Funny Garbage.

Peter's work has won numerous
awards, he's been invited to
speak around the world and
journalists have often covered
his projects in industry
magazines. Recent website
projects include the Cartoon
Network; David Byrne's world
music label Luaka Bop; A
re-design of the search engine
AltaVista; and an Interactive
Sesame Street on Web TV, for
Children's Television Workshop.

<Marcus Lynam>Creative Director-Webfactory

Webfactory, Ireland's 1998 Web Design Agency
of the Year, is recognized for its innovative
approach to technical and design projects and as
Creative Director, Marcus harnesses the talent of
his team to produce highly innovative Web
concepts and design. Marcus graduated from
D.L.I.A.D.T. Dublin, and worked in print design
and advertising, before discovering new media
and returning to college to explore its
possibilities. He was awarded a Masters Degree
from The Royal College of Art, London, in 1996.
Marcus has represented the Irish new media
industry as a committee member of ICAD
(Institute of Creative Advertising and Design)
and has been published in many international
design journals.

<Joe Duffy>President-Duffy Design

Joe heads up the design discipline for Fallon McElligott companies, through
Duffy Design and interactive. His work has won countless design awards
internationally and includes brand and corporate identity development
for leading companies such as Armani, BMW, Miller Brewing, Nordstrom,
McDonald's and Coca-Cola. Joe's understanding of how design affects
consumer attitudes has led to many big ideas executed in advertising,
as well as design. He has lectured on design throughout the U.S., Europe
and Australia.

</pageref>
<ix><rhp>

<Chris Briggs>Vice President, Brand Management Group-AGENCY.COM

As the vice president, creative director of brand management, Chris ensures that the AGENCY.COM brand is consistently represented across all forms of communication — from the company's Web site to fax forms. Previously as vice president, creative director of AGENCY.COM: New York, Chris managed the creative process to ensure that concepts were being integrated with technology to produce effective interactive business solutions for clients such as Sharp, Sprint and Hyatt Hotels and Resorts.

Chris was also one of the founders of CKS Interactive, a division of CKS Group, and Eagle River Interactive where he developed interactive multimedia applications for diverse clients, such as United Airlines, Apple Computers and McDonald's.

<John Grotting>Creative Director-Sapient

As Creative Director for Sapient, John helps build the firm's creative discipline in the East. He has led the design of the award-winning Kasparov vs. Deep Blue Web site, two evolutions of the IBM homepage as well as projects for Kodak and First Union. John attributes the complement of his design expertise and technical knowledge as the ingredients that attracted Motorola, Mercedes-Benz, Wells Fargo, and Nike to his own interactive design firm, Cow. John's work at Cow won widespread praise for graphic and interface design, including a Clio and awards from ID, Communication Arts, and Graphis.

<Wichar Jiempreecha>Senior Art Director-RareMedium

A master printmaker and still life painter, Wichar is a graduate of Bangkok's Silpakorn University and New York's School of Visual Arts Masters program in Computer Art. Throughout his career, Wichar has produced award-winning campaigns for clients such as Intel, Sprint, 3M, Philips, New York Lotto, Newsweek, Spin Magazine, Dow Jones, IBM, Disney, DC Comics and RCA. Other awards include Designer of the month by MS SiteBuilder Network, runner-up in the Truevision Video Graphics competition, first place award for best artistic video in the Truevision series, 1st place prize for 3-D fine art for "Turn of the Tide" and Grand Prize in the Computer Pictures Design Competition.

<Jan Ulrik Leth>Senior Partner/Executive Creative Director-Ogilvy Interactive

As Executive Creative Director of Ogilvy Interactive, New York, Jan has helped build a team that now numbers 140 people in NY alone and over 300 worldwide. Jan oversees all creative development for a growing list of blue-chip clients including IBM, GTE, Ford Motor Company, Perrier, Kodak, Lotus and Tivoli. Ogilvy Interactive has won numerous awards including a Gold CyberLion, Caples, Adtech, One Show and Effies. Jan's other awards include: Gold Echo for British Airways, Gold Echo for Oxford Health Plans, Gold Effie for Oxford, 1st place Caples for Cigna. Jan has also served as a judge for the One Show, the Andy Awards, Adtech, Caples and the Echoes.

<Joel Hladecek>Partner & Chief Creative Director-Red Sky Interactive

With his background in the film, special effects and motion picture ride industry, Joel is the major impetus behind Red Sky Interactive's signature creative. As chief creative director, Joel oversees the company's creative team on its many notable projects including the award-winning CD-ROM "Red Sky on the Frontier" and the "HP Pong" ad banner that have both won MC Icon Awards. Before joining Red Sky, Joel was a motion-control camera operator and special effects supervisor for Matte World in Novato, California and has judged several industry events in the interactive field including the Clios and the Communications Arts Interactive Annual.

</pageref>
<x><lhp>

<Tom Nicholson>President and Chief Executive Officer-Nicholson NY

Under Tom Nicholson's creative and strategic leadership, Nicholson NY has developed highly acclaimed work for the country's leading technology, media, automotive, pharmaceutical and financial services companies. With project teams that draw from more than 90 top strategists, designers, technologists, media experts and researchers, the agency is a leading provider of interactive and e-commerce solutions. Tom himself remains one of the most sought-after creative leaders in the world of digital media. He currently serves on the Advisory Board of the Center for Advanced Technologies at New York University. His work has been featured in leading design and news magazines including The New York Times, Time Magazine, I.D. Magazine and Print.

<Stephen Embleton>Creative Director-Armadillo Interactive

Starting as a designer for Matthews & Charter, Stephen points to 1996 as the year he learned how to make something mundane pulsate with energy using pure design, as well as the year he was introduced to THE INTERNET. Stephen describes Internet design as a world of "non-print, non-paint," yet he applies what he learned in print to interactive work, creating endless possibilities in a communication medium offering animation, sound and unlimited colors regardless of a client's budget. As Creative Director for Armadillo Interactive, Stephen focuses his attention on what he calls the "young, naive and innocent" market of South African interactive design.

<Dave Parrish>V.P., Creative Partner-Martin Interactive

In 1995, Dave began his interactive career developing the first Web site for Coca-Cola. Since then, Dave has used his creative direction and vision to develop online marketing for other brands such as Saab, Gerber, Rémy Martin, Marriott, Seiko/Pulsar and FMC. Dave has won the prestigious One Show award for his work on Coca-Cola, SURGE, and Rémy Martin. He has also been recognized by Graphis, The N.Y. Art Directors Show and The Richmond Show. Dave began his career with The Martin Agency in 1988 where his client roster included accounts such as SkyTel, CompuServe, GEICO, Sprint, US WEST and FMC.

<Dan Olson>Creative Director-Revolv

As Creative Director for Revolv, the new media division of Fallon McElligott and Duffy Design, Don Olson has designed interactive projects for clients such as BMW, Ralston Purina, Nikon, United Airlines and Qualcomm.

His work has been widely recognized by both national and international design and advertising competitions such as: Communication Arts, Graphis, The American Center for Design, The Art Directors Club of New York, American Institute of Graphic Artists and The One Show. Dan also serves as adjunct faculty at the College of Visual Arts in St. Paul, Minnesota and contributed to design workshops at the Minneapolis College of Art and Design.

<Andrew Sather>Senior Vice President-Sapient

In 1995, Andrew Sather founded Adjacency to ensure that great brands define and dominate their categories online. Today, in his role as a leader in Sapient's creative discipline, Andrew helps to set creative strategy and evolve design, information architecture, brand strategy and content development's place within the company's multidisciplinary development methodology.

Trained as a graphic designer and writer, Andrew recognized early on the potential for the Internet to transform brand-building, design, communication and commerce. Working with creative director Bernie DeChant, Andrew has co-led the conception and design of Adjacency-created Web sites including new or revised Web presences and e-commerce platforms for clients like Nordstrom, Apple Computer, Patagonia, Specialized, Adobe, TAG Heuer, Caterpillar and Virgin.

</pageref>
<xi><rhp>

Power windows...

Click here

Power door locks... cruise control...

Click here

The 1999 4Runner

Click here

TOYOTA | *everyday*

Click here

>

<html>
<head>

<category>	Banner-Link Only Single</head>
<award>	Gold</title>
<agency>	Saatchi & Saatchi/Los Angeles
<client>	Toyota Motor Sales/USA
<url>	www.saatchila.com/extras/oneshow/
<art director>	Laura Rhoads
<writer>	John Diggins
<producer>	Matt Mayer
<programmer>	Eric Gieszl
<creative directors>	Chris Ray Dean Van Eimeren
<hardware>	Apple Macintosh
<software>	Adobe Photoshop Adobe ImageReady Gif Builder

</frameset>
<noframes>

<a parody> The challenge was to create online advertisements that were relevant to the interactive medium. A parody of an alert window seemed a logical solution. The key to making "Download" work visually was to emulate the way a computer downloads a file, with many elements transferring rapidly while other elements seemed to choke the download process. This was also an ideal opportunity to highlight specific equipment features on the 4Runner. "Download" became the first of many similar dialogue box treatments, all of which have been popular as well as effective.

</pageref>
<1><rhp>

<award>
<Silver> </pic>
<head>
<category>Banner-Link Only Single</head>

Does your monitor *s t i n k ?*

Click here.

<html>
<head>

<category>	Banner-Link Only Single</head>	
<award>	Silver</title>	
<agency>	Messner Vetere Berger McNamee Schmetterer/Euro RSCG/New York	
<client>	Philips	
<url>	www.clients.mvbms.com/oneshow/ (login: oneshow, password: awards)	
<art director>	Eric Peterson	
<writer>	Drew Burchenal	
<producer>	Chris Murphy	
<creative director>	Jason Lellos	
<hardware>	Apple Macintosh	
<software>	Adobe Illustrator Adobe Photoshop Macromedia Flash Macromedia Director	

</frameset>
<noframes>

<go monitor
shopping>

<stodgy to innovative>

Sometimes the simplest concept is the best concept. This banner is an example of that principle. We had a unique challenge, in that we were trying to sell monitors to people who were looking at monitors when they saw the ad. We couldn't show the actual product benefit, because their viewing experience was restricted by the limitations of their monitor. Instead, we decided to use a humorous concept to persuade the audience that it was time to go monitor shopping.

This banner was trafficked with a background color that matched the pages on which it appeared. This made the borders of the banner disappear into the page. In doing this, we hoped people wouldn't realize at first they were seeing a banner. The Fly bounces across the screen for a few seconds before the copy pay-off comes in. Copy is short and to the point, driving traffic to the Philips Monitor Site.

The banner is unbranded to build intrigue. Though it took some time to convince the client to go with the idea, it ended up being very successful. It was the first step in helping Philips update its image, from outdated and stodgy to innovative and fun.

</pageref>
<2><thp>

Dear Santa-
How do you get around the world so fast?
Love, Sally

Dear Sally - TCI @Home. Love, Santa

Click here for Internet cheer up to 100 times faster. TCI @ Home

>

<html>
<head>

<category>	Banner-Link Only Single</head>	
<award>	Bronze</title>	
<agency>	Click Here/Dallas	
<client>	TCI@Home	
<url>	www.clickhere.com/oneshow/santa/remote	
<art director>	Jim Kuenzer	
<writer>	Jim Kuenzer	
<programmer>	Jim Kuenzer	
<hardware>	Apple Macintosh	
<software>	Adobe ImageReady	
</frameset>		
<noframes>		

<years of inquiry> When I was a kid, I never questioned Santa's motives, why his elves would shrink wrap toys or even his ability to squeeze down a chimney (we lived in a house with no fireplace and still got presents, obviously Santa used windows, too). No, I doubted anyone could ever get around the world in one night, Rudolph or not. So after years of inquiry and investigation, postulating and theorizing, I decided to get Sally to ask Santa the big question. What have I learned? Santa is an illusive smarty pants.

</pageref>
<3><rhp>

<award>

<Gold>  </pic>

Microsoft® Windows® 98 radically accelerates your access to your favorite applications. It does this by figuring out what programs you use most and rearranging them at a tiny micro level to be quicker and more efficient. So you barely have time to say,

"SHEESH, THAT'S A LOT FASTER."

Works better. Plays better.

In fact, an average of *36% faster*. So why don't you relax a little and read at a more leisurely pace. Let your operating system do the hurrying.

■ CLICK TO ORDER
■ MICROSOFT® WINDOWS® 98 WEB SITE
■ CLICK FOR *MORE>* DISK SPACE

<html>
<head>

<category>	Banner-Link Only Campaign</head>
<award>	Gold</title>
agency>	Wieden & Kennedy/New York
<client>	Microsoft
<url>	www.wk.com/newbiz/
<art directors>	Kevin Drew Davis Jon Stoa
<writer>	Bill Weinstein
<digital artists>	Heather Hadlock Terry Keenan
<producer>	Katie Raye
<programmer>	Michael Macrone
<creative directors>	Kevin Drew Davis Bob Moore Michael Prieve
<hardware>	Apple Macintosh PC
<software>	Adobe Illustrator Adobe ImageReady Adobe Photoshop

</frameset>
<noframes>

</pageref>
<4><ihp>

OPENS PROGRAMS 36% FASTER

OPENS PROGRAMS 36% FASTER

MICROSOFT® WINDOWS® 98.
CLICK FOR **MORE>** SPEED.

SUDDENLY YOU HAVE 28% MORE DISK SPACE.

>

<individual benefits>

For the launch of Windows 98, Wieden &
Kennedy created a series of banners
targeted to the home-PC user. Instead
of trying to build a site that explained
every benefit, the campaign focused on
individual benefits users would appreciate
in their daily computer usage.
Simple things like: "more disk space,"
"faster," "USB support," and "automatic
maintenance." The banner animations
were intended to highlight the benefit
being promoted.

</pageref>
5 <rhp>

ALERO
CLICK TO START SOMETHING

START FEELING CONNECTED

ALERO
ACTIVE RESPONSE SYSTEM

WIN! RUB ELBOWS WITH NBA STARS' KNEES

WIN! CLICK TO WIN A NEW ALERO AND AN ESPY AWARDS VACATION

WIN! ALERO START SOMETHING ONLINE SWEEPSTAKES

<html>
<head>

<category>	Banner-Link Only Campaign</head>
<award>	Silver</title>
<agency>	Giant Step/Chicago
<client>	Oldsmobile Alero
<art director>	Sean Moran
<digital artists>	Sean Moran Paul Kraus Eric Bailey Brian Pentecost
<producer>	Christine Saxman
<multimedia>	Geoff Petkus
<programmers>	Geoff Petkus Sunil Taneja Rich Dominquez Mike Parker
<hardware>	Apple Macintosh PC
<software>	Adobe Illustrator Adobe Photoshop Macromedia Flash Microsoft Visual Studio

</frameset>
<noframes>

</pageref>
<6><lhp>

<100 million impressions> At the beginning of 1998, Giant Step and its client Oldsmobile started to see impressive results from the company's online marketing efforts. Fueled by this success, Giant Step assembled one of the largest Internet media campaigns ever launched by an automobile manufacturer. By the end of the campaign, Alero would garner nearly 100 million impressions across top Internet Web sites.

<never seen the car> The campaign had two goals. The first was to introduce the all-new Alero to an Internet audience that had never seen the car before. The second was to drive traffic to startsomething.com, a sweepstakes site that would provide Oldsmobile with information about its target market.

<a tighter bond> The campaign was a resounding success on both fronts. The campaign built brand awareness by featuring a photograph of the Alero in each of 175 unique banner designs. In addition, the majority of the banner concepts harmonized with the subject matter on the sites, providing a tighter bond between content and advertising for the audience.

</pageref>
<7><rhp>

<award>
<Bronze>  </pic>

NationsBank Online

Secure

NationsBank Online

Easy

NationsBank Online

Free

NationsBank Online

<html>
<head>

<category>	Banner-Link Only Campaign</head>
<award>	Bronze</title>
<agency>	Lot21 Interactive Advertising/San Francisco
<client>	NationsBank
<url>	www.lot21.com/public/osi/nationsbank/
<programmer>	Sasha Pave
<creative director>	Paco Vinoly
<hardware>	Apple Macintosh
<software>	Adobe Photoshop Macromedia Fireworks Macromedia Flash

</frameset>
<noframes>

</pageref>
<8><lhp>

Take Control
of Your Finances

Direct Access to Your Accounts
NationsBank
Online

<competitive advantage> In the NationsBank Flash banner campaign the challenge for Lot21 was finding new ways to market NationsBank Financial Services that cut through the ample "noise" that exists on the Web, while not taking on excess risk, so that acquisitions and profitability could be optimized. Understanding the demographics of online bankers created a competitive advantage of predicting customer behavior.

<varying scenarios> Creative had to meet the needs and wants of consumers on a one-to-one basis to attract current and potential customers online given varying scenarios of financial service offerings. The campaign achieved this by enhancing NationsBank's brand and services in a profoundly complimentary design.

<prominent branding> The functionality of Macromedia Flash allowed Lot21's design team to create high-impact visual effects while keeping the animations to a very reasonable file size. The clean, crisp visuals, along with consistent and prominent branding, were of utmost importance.

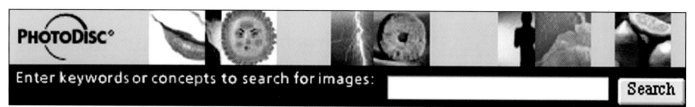

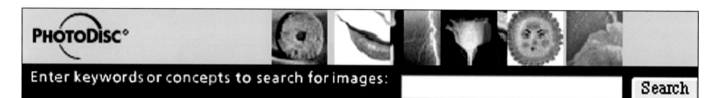

<html>
<head>

<category>	Banner-Interactive Single</head>
<award>	Gold</title>
<agency>	Hyperinteractive/London
<client>	Photodisc
<url>	www.hyperinteractive.com/photodisc2.html
<art directors>	Richard Mellor Siba Torbati
<programmer>	Siba Torbati
<hardware>	Apple Macintosh
<software>	Macromedia Director Macromedia Shockwave

</frameset>
<noframes>

<put a man on the moon>

With a dimension of 486 x 60 pixels, a maximum data size of 15K, and a limited pallet of 256 colors, it makes you wonder how anyone could ever create a stimulating interactive banner for an image library. However, the "Speed" Photodisc banner challenges these limitations in a highly imaginative manner. Furthermore, concealing more processing power than it took to put a man on the moon, it also doubles up as a powerful image search engine.

<pick an image, any image!>

Emulating the shuffle motions of a pack of playing cards, each image deals, dances, flies and flicks back and forth. As an additional play element, the speed and the direction of the motion is also influenced by the position of the cursor. This creates a feeling of interaction at its most playful, funniest and dynamic. The end result was well worth the effort. After all, as they say "...a picture tells a thousand words," but a highly hypnotic, cursor-sensitive, image-searching, all-dancing, interactive banner will always be worth more than a thousand pictures—75,000 of them, to be precise.

</pageref>
<10><lhp>

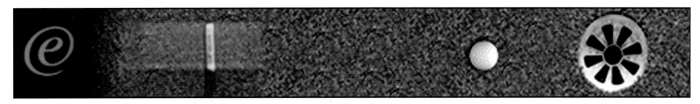

 www.pga.com is an IBM e-business.
Click here and drop in.

<html>
<head>

<category>	Banner-Interactive Single</head>
<award>	Silver</title>
<agency>	Ogilvy Interactive/New York
<client>	IBM
<url>	www.oandmi.com/media/eculture/work/showcase.html (username: media, password: banners)
<art director>	Warren Kemp
<writer>	David Levy
<digital artist>	Rachael Heapps
<producers>	Jude Raymond Fish Kate Kehoe
<programmer>	David Carson/Compound
<creative director>	Jan Leth
<hardware>	Apple Macintosh
<software>	Adobe Illustrator Adobe Photoshop Enliven Macromedia Director Macromedia Flash

</frameset>
<noframes>

<a testimonial> The cursor as putter. Tap the golf ball into the cup (it actually takes a bit of finesse) and you're rewarded with that satisfying sound familiar to any golfer—and a teaser to PGA's e-business interstitial: a testimonial to IBM's expertise in building a compelling Web site for PGA's rabid fans.

</pageref>
<11><rhp>

   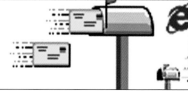

<html>

<head>

<category>	Banner-Interactive Single</head>
<award>	Bronze</title>
<agency>	Anderson & Lembke/San Francisco
<client>	Microsoft
<url>	www.anlsf.com/oneshow/ oe_game/index.html
<art director>	Megan McMahon
<writer>	John Pinson
<producer>	Alyson Kohn
<programmers>	Chris Hurwitz Art Boterell
<creative directors>	Glen Sheehan Bill Day
<hardware>	Apple Macintosh PC
<software>	Adobe Photoshop Macromedia Director Adobe Illustrator BBEdit

</frameset>

<noframes>

<catch "e-mail," avoid spam">

(Sorry, but this book isn't compatible with Shockwave plug-in version 7.01. So you'll have to grab an art director, some scissors and a stapler to make this thing work.)

Directions for making a flip-book:
1) Cut out all of the frames. 2) Staple them together on the left side. 3) Grab the left side of book firmly and flip rapidly through the pages. 4) Once you get a smooth animation going, pretend your fingertip is your cursor and place it over the mailbox. 5) Raise and lower your mailbox, trying to catch "e-mail" and avoid "spam."

<itchy mouse finger>

Congratulations. You have just been immersed in a product benefit demonstration. The idea that Outlook Express will help you avoid all of that annoying spam has been set in your mind while you were busy having fun. You come away with greater awareness. Brand perception. Heightened hand-eye coordination. And, if you're like a lot of other people with an itchy mouse finger and an aversion to spam, your very own version of Outlook Express.

<award>
<Bronze>  </pic>

<head>
<category>Banner-Interactive Single</head>

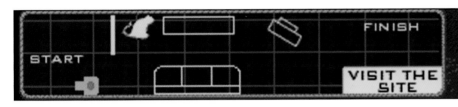

<html>
<head>

<category>	Banner-Interactive Single</head>
<award>	Bronze</title>
<agency>	APL Digital/New York
<client>	Lego
<writer>	Jay Zasa
<digital artist>	Khoi Le
<producer>	Jenny Howell
<programmer>	Bruce Ledbetter
<creative director>	Evan Lewis
<hardware>	Apple Macintosh
<software>	Macromedia Director Narrative Enliven Extra

</frameset>
<noframes>

</pageref>
<13><rhp>

<award>
<Gold>  </pic>

 Air Canada and IBM. Tickets to ride. Online. }
Click here and fly there.

 www.pga.com is an IBM e-business.
Click here and drop in.

<html>
<head>

<category>	Banner-Interactive Campaign</head>
<award>	Gold</title>
<agency>	Ogilvy Interactive/New York
<client>	IBM
<url>	www.oandmi.com/media/eculture/work/showcase.html (username: media, password: banners)
<art directors>	Warren Kemp Juan Gallardo
<writer>	David Levy
<digital artists>	Rachael Heapps Terrance Peng Pamela Mitchell
<producers>	Jude Raymond Fish Kate Kehoe
<programmer>	David Carson/Compound
<creative director>	Jan Leth
<hardware>	Apple Macintosh
<software>	Adobe Illustrator Adobe Photoshop Enliven Macromedia Director Macromedia Flash

</frameset>
<noframes>

</pageref>
<14><lhp>

<energize their business>
Our goal with this campaign was to show how IBM e-business solutions have helped a range of companies energize their businesses by taking advantage of the Internet. The broader intention was to tout how Internet-based solutions (with IBM leading the way) have pervaded countless aspects of contemporary life—from making airline reservations on the Web to hiking in boots bought from an online store.

<pushing the electronic envelope>
Each company had its own unique e-business solution so it was important that each story—though unmistakably IBM—had a feel of its own. And since e-business is all about pushing the electronic envelope, so to speak, it was necessary to do the same with this campaign.

<a bit of fun>
The banners work, one hopes, by offering a bit of fun before the serious sell. We created a series of interactive visual metaphors, such as the one for REI, a retailer of outdoor gear, in which the cursor becomes a "flashlight" helping the user search for a campsite, and the copy talks about helping your business "find its way to the Web."

<overall look>
As for the overall look, the banners follow the lead of the IBM print and broadcast work. For the testimonial pop-ups, key colors were extracted from each customer's Web site. We wanted to keep these pop-ups free of clutter—to give the imagery as much breathing room as possible without overwhelming the top-line message.

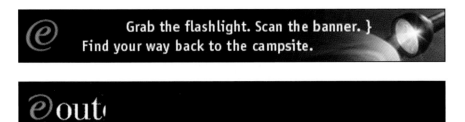

Grab the flashlight. Scan the banner. }
Find your way back to the campsite.

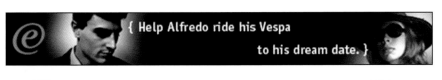

It called some experts to shed some light on the subject
Click here to see how

{ Help Alfredo ride his Vespa
to his dream date. }

IBM AND VESPA PUT THE BUZZ ONLINE.

Objective ▶ Bring the romance of Italy's Vespa scooters
Solution ▶ to a global audience. And improve
Results ▶ communication within the company.

Continue story ▶

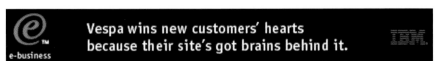

Vespa wins new customers' hearts
because their site's got brains behind it.

THE 21ST CENTURY PLAYER PIANO.

Objective ▶ Promote the company's Disklavier,
Solution ▶ a modern-day "player piano" that
Results ▶ performs music from digital files.

Continue story ▶

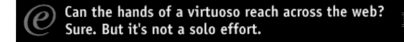

Can the hands of a virtuoso reach across the web?
Sure. But it's not a solo effort.

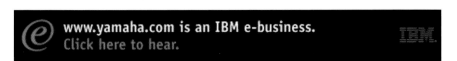

www.yamaha.com is an IBM e-business.
Click here to hear.

</pageref>
<15><rhp>

\<html\>
\<head\>

\<html\>	\<category\>	Banner-Interactive Campaign\</head\>
\<head\>	\<award\>	Silver\</title\>
	\<agency\>	Grey Interactive/Helsinki
	\<client\>	Paulig
	\<url\>	www.greyinteractive.fi/oneshow/ paulig/index.htm
	\<art director\>	Vainionpaa Marja
	\<writer\>	Liisa Vahakyla
	\<producers\>	Anita Laaksonen Jaana Komulainen
	\<programmer\>	Ala-aho Klaus
	\<hardware\>	Apple Macintosh PC
	\<software\>	Adobe Photoshop UltraEdit html-editor Ulead GifAnimator

\</frameset\>
\<noframes\>
\<br\>\<br\>

\<coffee lovers\>

The first objective of this online campaign was to activate the target group—young urban coffee lovers—thereby strengthening the brand image of Paulig special coffees. The banners were presented in online media geared toward younger audiences. The secondary objective was to support the "classic" campaign, which ran simultaneously in print and outdoor. The URL was in that advertising as well.

\<e-mail postcards\>

The campaign pages contained information on Paulig special coffees, as well as some selected recipes and the capability of sending e-mail postcards. The campaign consisted of three banners, presented visitors in a personal carousel in a certain order. The banner contained more than one link: visitors could go either straight to the Paulig pages or to the e-card page. Interactivity was emphasized by the postcard-sending feature. The postcard itself contained alternative texts and free-text fields, so one could choose what kind of message to send to invite a friend for a cup of coffee. The point of the postcards, of course, was to help spread awareness.

\<br\>

</pageref>
<17><rhp>

\<category\>	Banner-Interactive Campaign</head>
\<award\>	Bronze</title>
\<agency\>	Modem Media.Poppe Tyson/Chicago
\<client\>	3Com
\<art director\>	Steven Cloud
\<writers\>	Kent Molyneaux Steve Tullis
\<digital artist\>	Kelly Wottrich
\<producer\>	Michael Borsari
\<programmers\>	Dave Whalen Michael Borsari
\<creative director\>	Charles Marrelli
\<hardware\>	Apple Macintosh PC
\<software\>	Adobe Illustrator Adobe Photoshop Equilibrium Debabilizer Gif Builder Java

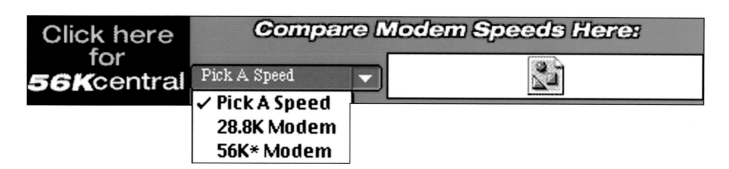

<"experience" the difference>

This banner campaign communicated a powerful message to 28.8K modem users by allowing them to actually "experience" the difference of a 56K modem. Using media-rich technology, viewers were invited to interact with the message and see for themselves how the Web works with a US Robotics 56K modem from 3Com.

<these three banners>

The banners were placed on tech-savvy Web sites and other mainstream areas of the Web. The average click-through rate was 5.4% with an average interaction rate of 40%. In a six-week flight period, these three banners delivered more than 250,000 visitors to a Web site called "56K Central."

</pageref>
<19><rhp>

>WRITE JAVA APPS WITHOUT WRITING CODE. CLICK HERE.

Sun
microsystems

PLEASE WAIT...LOADING IMAGES & AUDIO

INSTRUCTIONS:
DRAG ICONS FROM THE
RIGHT-HAND SIDE OF
THE SCREEN INTO
THE STORY.

\<html\>
\<head\>

\<category\>	Beyond the Banner\</head\>
\<award\>	Gold\</title\>
\<agency\>	Lowe & Partners/SMS/New York, San Francisco
\<client\>	Sun Microsystems
\<url\>	38.245.119.101/sun/web/development.html
\<art director\>	J. Kent Pepper
\<writer\>	Andrew Baker
\<producer\>	John Bains
\<multimedia\>	Lateral Net/London
\<programmer\>	Lee Coomber
\<creative directors\>	Lee Garfinkel
	Gary Goldsmith
	Peter Cohen
	Dean Hacohen
\<hardware\>	Apple Macintosh, PC
\<software\>	Adobe Photoshop, Java Development Tools
	Macromedia Director

\</frameset\>
\</pageref\>   \<noframes\>
\<20\>\<lhp\>   \<br\>\<br\>
\<br\>\<br\>

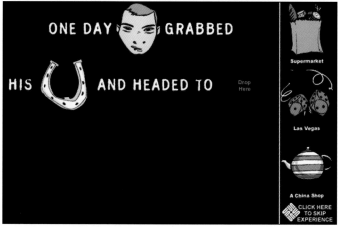

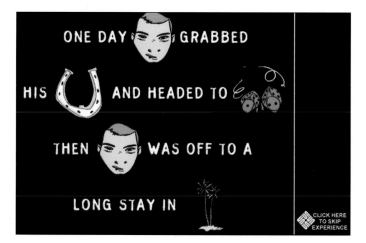

<because of its promise> Target: Developers and Content Managers. They are technically sophisticated software programmers and they already have a strong interest in Java technology because of its promise of "write once, run anywhere" as opposed to writing a long string of redundant code.

<interesting storytelling> Synopsis/Objectives: Sun, the creator of Java technology, provides fast and easy-to-use Java development and authoring tools that harness the full potential of Java "write once, run anywhere." Java is much faster as a programming language than C++ or any other coding language. This banner and jump page demonstrate Java's speed in an interesting storytelling format.

</pageref>
<21><rhp>

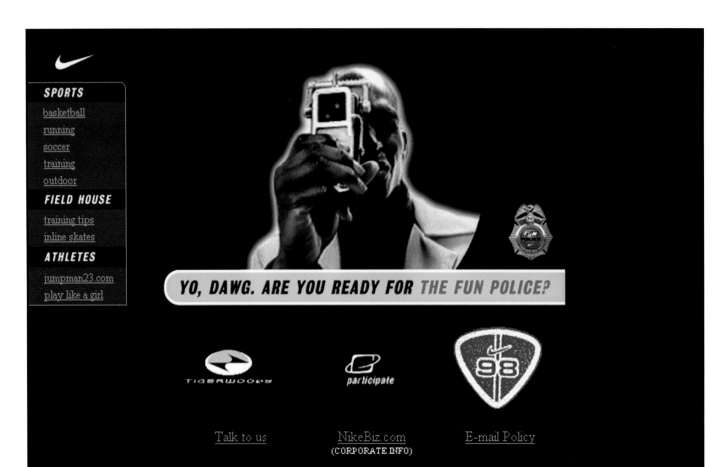

\<category\>	Beyond the Banner\</head\>
\<award\>	Silver\</title\>
\<agency\>	Wieden & Kennedy/New York
\<client\>	Nike
\<url\>	www.wk.com/newbiz/
\<art directors\>	Kevin Drew Davis Guthrie Dolin Mike Maketil
\<writers\>	Jamie Barrett Derek Barnes
\<digital artist\>	Linda Reynen
\<producer\>	Katie Raye
\<multimedia\>	SF Interactive
\<programmers\>	Jacob Davies Matisse Enzer Michael Macrone
\<creative directors\>	Kevin Drew Davis Jamie Barrett John Jay
\<hardware\>	Unix
\<software\>	Adobe Illustrator, Adobe ImageReady Adobe Photoshop, CGI, PERL

<the fun police>   To extend the Fun Police television campaign, Wieden & Kennedy created a mini-site on nike.com utilizing elements from the previous television campaign (the Fun Cave, Gadgetry, Nicknames, Fun/Not Fun tests).

<nicknames and favorite colors>   Upon registering, the user was given a nickname and greeted by their favorite player. The site even kept track of the user's favorite color and personalized the site with it. Every time they visited the site, a pop-up window appeared asking the user to rate the "fun-ness" of various activities or things.

<a series of missions>   The core of the site is a series of missions where users must answer funny trivia questions about basketball, Fun Police members and details of the Fun Police television spots. Correct answers prompt congratulations from the user's favorite player. Wrong answers prompt a series of hints from their favorite player.

</pageref>
<23><rhp>

<award>
<Bronze>  </pic>

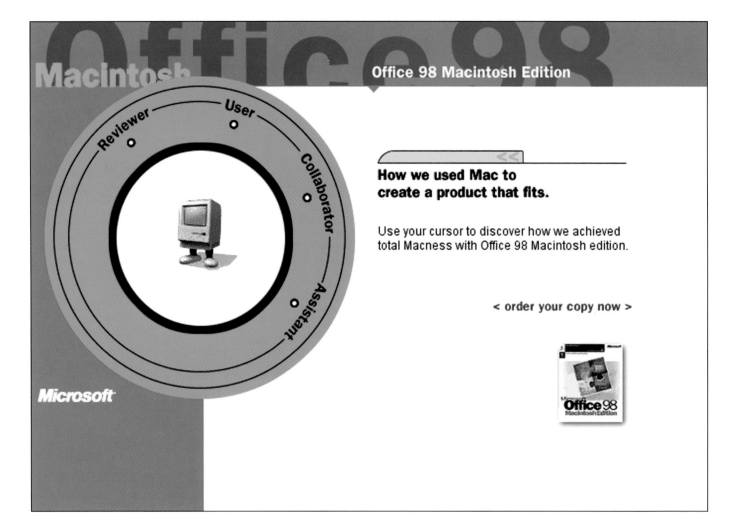

<html>
<head>

<category>	Beyond the Banner</head>
<award>	Bronze</title>
<agency>	Anderson & Lembke/San Francisco
<client>	Microsoft
<url>	www.anlsf.com/oneshow
<art director>	Matthew Schneider
<writer>	Steve Scowden
<digital artists>	Mark French Tom Ran
<producer>	Daniel Stein
<programmer>	David Thibodeau
<creative directors>	Glen Sheehan Bill Day
<hardware>	Apple Macintosh
<software>	Adobe Illustrator Adobe Photoshop BBEdit Motion Works Camerman

</frameset>
<noframes>

</pageref>
<24><lhp>

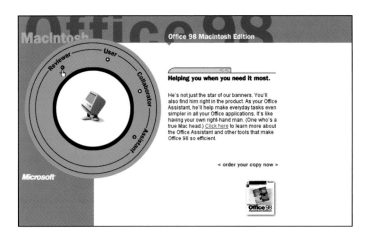

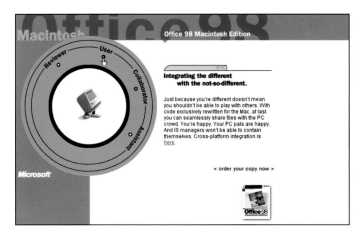

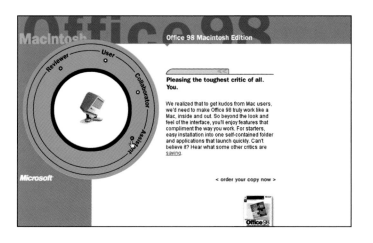

\<picture this\>   You're creative or you wouldn't be reading these things. So picture this. You're sitting in front of your Mac. Surfing the Web. A banner shows up asking you to "Imagine all your applications built entirely in your own image." Then a cute little Mac walks out and looks at itself in a mirror. You gotta click.

\<trying to tell you\>   You arrive at the Microsoft MacOffice microsite and there's that cute little Mac again, looking out at you. Wait, what's this? The little guy starts to give you attitude, tapping its foot impatiently. Then it collapses onto the floor in frustration. Okay, so maybe it's trying to tell you something. (Like, hurry up and do something.) So you mouse over to the navigation that surrounds the Mac. He watches your cursor as it rolls over the choices.

\<the path to consideration\>   You click on "Assistant" for kicks and discover the "Assistant" is the little Mac with the attitude. And he comes with MacOffice. Cool. You click on the text link, and off you go into the Microsoft MacOffice site, tapping your foot and speeding down the path to consideration.

\<br\>

\>

<award>
<Gold> </pic>

<html>
<head>

<category>	Promotional Advertising-Web Sites</head>
<award>	Gold</title>
<agency>	DoubleYou/Barcelona
<client>	Audi/Spain
<url>	audi.vw-audi.es/tt/
<art director>	Blanca Piera
<writer>	Esther Pino
<digital artists>	Joakim Borgström Oriol Quin
<producer>	David Esteve
<programmer>	Joakim Borgström
<creative director>	Daniel Solana
<hardware>	Apple Macintosh PC
<software>	Adobe Illustrator, Adobe Photoshop Allaire Home Site, Gif Builder Macromedia Fireworks Ulead Gif Animator

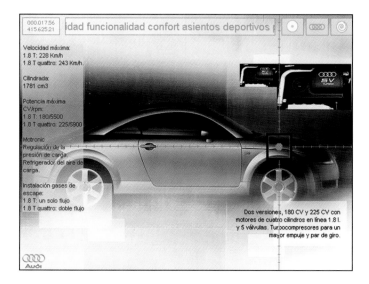

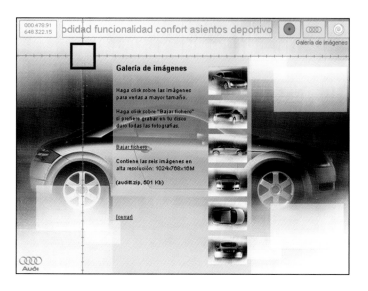

<design, instinct and technology>

This minisite was specially created for the release of the new Audi TT in Spain, using design, instinct and technology as its main concepts. Created for potential consumers of Audi, those interested in new car designs and anyone yearning for the best design and technology, the site shows the characteristics of the new Audi model via non-linear browsing according to the user's interest.

<requirements of the user>

The site contains a visual and interactive description of the new Audi TT and discusses the concepts of the car: equipment, air conditioning, engine, alarm, interior design and other details. A welcome page has all content contained in a single interface and information appears according to the requirements of the user. Rollovers on the image of the Audi TT causes informative text, characteristic techniques, detailed photographs and additional information to appear in dynamic pop-up windows. Three additional buttons in the top right corner contain a gallery of photos, a place to play the TV spot and a direct link to the Audi Web site.

</pageref>
<27><rhp>

<award>
<Gold> </pic>

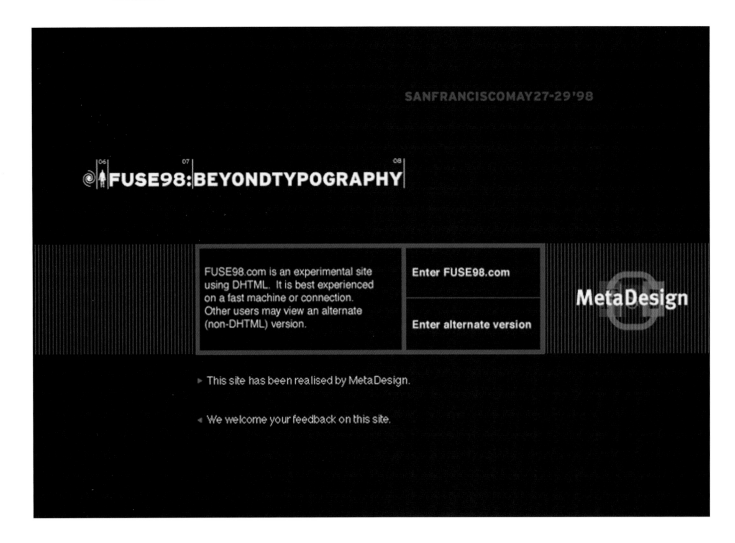

<html>
<head>

<category>	Promotional Advertising-Web Sites</head>
<award>	Gold</title>
<agency>	MetaDesign/San Francisco
<client>	Fuse Conferences
<url>	www.fuse98.com
<art directors>	Rick Lowe Olivier Chetelat Shawn Hazen Eva Walter
<writers>	Christopher Myers Shel Perkins David Peters Rhonda Rubinstein
<photographer>	Ligia Dias
<producer>	David Peters
<programmer>	Joseph Ternes
<hardware>	Apple Macintosh PC
<software>	Adobe Illustrator, Adobe Photoshop BBEdit, Fetch, GifBuilder

</frameset>
</pageref> <noframes>
<28><lhp>

<catalyze a new vision>

FUSE98.com was created as a channel for information about FUSE98: Beyond Typography, an international design event presented in San Francisco by MetaDesign, in conjunction with Neville Brody and FontShop International.
The event sought to catalyze a new vision of the communications world and renew our understanding of the technological context in which that world is embedded. The Web site became an electronic extension of the conference and features FUSE98Lab, a test area/gallery for digital experiments. More than twenty projects were selected from submissions by designers all over the world, and range from a randomized business card generator to interactive poetry.

<search for meaning>

With FUSE98 the Web team had the opportunity to design a site geared towards savvy designers with high technology, high bandwidth systems.
It was also a chance to seize the emerging capabilities of DHTML and to design an interface using a one-page metaphor, allowing full access to information without the distractions of full-screen re-loads. This single page presents a layering of content which the user can access simply by "pulling" information to the fore. This concept furthered the conference's theme of the search for meaning in the onslaught of today's information society. The "home page" of FUSE98.com is thus "all the information at once."

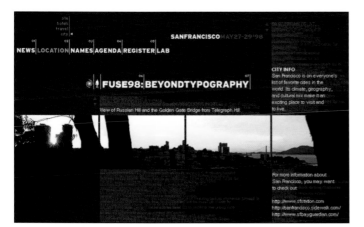

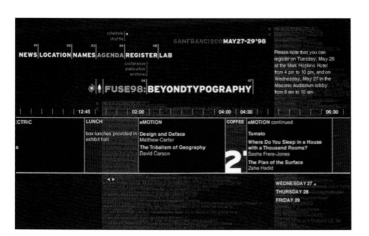

</pageref>
<29><rhp>

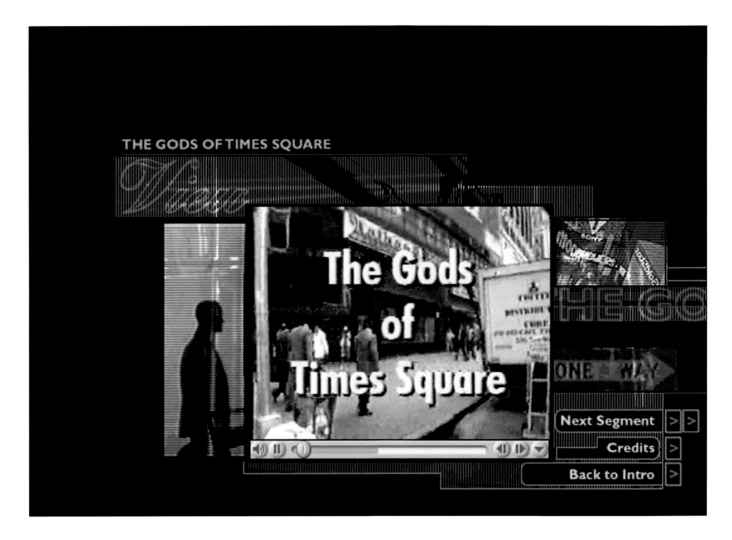

<html>
<head>

<category>	Promotional Advertising–Web Sites</head>
<award>	Silver</title>
<agency>	AGENCY.COM/New York
<client>	Urban Desires
<url>	www.desires.com/features/gts/
<art director>	PJ Loughran
<writer>	Richard Sandler
<digital artist>	Tom Moran
<producers>	Kiley Bates
	James Plath
	Kyle Shannon
	Chan Suh
	Gabrielle Shannon
	Richard Sandler
	Mary Bosakowski
	Dan Brown
<programmer>	Dheeraj Vasishta
<creative director>	PJ Loughran
<hardware>	Apple Macintosh, PC
<software>	Adobe ImageReady, Adobe Photoshop
	Quicktime, Java

</frameset>
</pageref>
30><lhp>   <noframes>

<a new landscape> My first experience with New York was like encountering a new landscape filled with motion, sound, shape, color, intensity. Unexpected urban beauty. The energy, the noise, the crowds, the heights, dizzying in their depth and complexity and speed and detail all worked to redefine my vision of urban beauty.

<the framework> These ideas and emotions form the frame-work of the design in which "The Gods of Times Square" expresses its voice—the life of New York through my eyes.

</pageref>
<31><rhp>

<award>
<Bronze>   </pic>

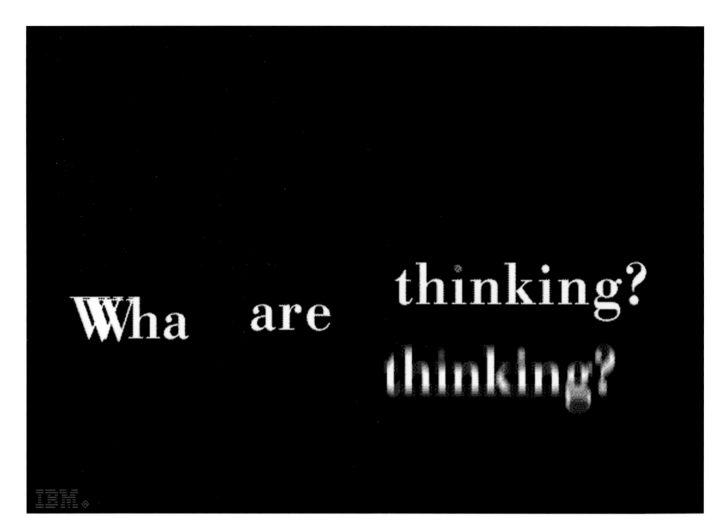

<html>
<head>

<category>	Promotional Advertising-Web Sites</head>
<award>	Bronze</title>
<agency>	CKS Partners/Portland
<client>	IBM
<url>	pdx.cks.com/thinkpad600/think_highband
<art director>	Richard Dunn
<writer>	James Cheung
<digital artist>	Richard Dunn
<photographer>	Damian Conrad
<producer>	Richard Dunn
<programmer>	Richard Dunn
<creative director>	Russ Hoffman
<hardware>	Apple Macintosh
<software>	Adobe Photoshop Macromedia Director Macromedia Shockwave

</frameset>
<noframes>

</pageref>
<32><lhp>

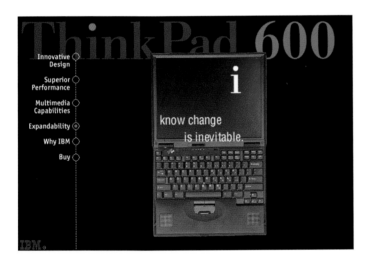

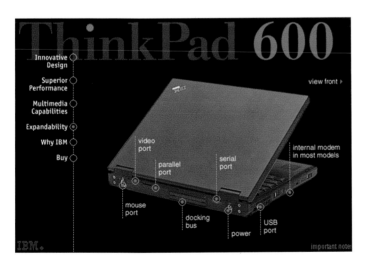

<for your buck> Think big. Big bang. Big splash. Big stuff. Wow. It's out of sight. It's dynamite. It's alright. IBM THINKPAD 600. A lot of power in a small package. More bang for your buck. Very lightweight. Ultimate technology. Shock the eyes. Shock the ears. Shock the fingers. You wouldn't have more fun if you had a punchbowl at this party.

</pageref>
<33><rhp>

A Centenary Celebration of the Life & Work of the Artist John Gilroy

\<html>
\<head>

\<category>	Promotional Advertising-Web Sites\</head>
\<award>	Bronze\</title>
\<agency>	Webfactory/Dublin
\<client>	Guinness
\<url>	www.guinness-gilroy.com/
\<art director>	Marcus Lynam
\<writer>	Catherine Feeney
\<digital artist>	Richard Pittham
\<producer>	Simon Walsh
\<multimedia>	Webfactory
\<programmer>	Niall Colgan
\<hardware>	Apple Macintosh, PC
\<software>	Adobe Illustrator
	Adobe ImageReady
	Adobe Photoshop
	Equilibrium DeBabelizer
	Macromedia Dreamweaver
	Macromedia Fireworks
	Macromedia Freehand
	Specular Infini-D

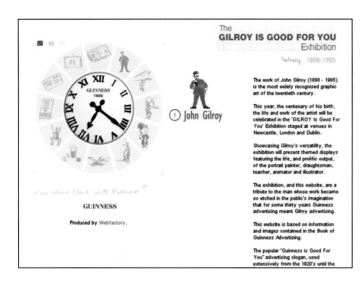

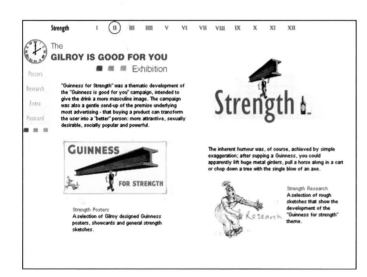

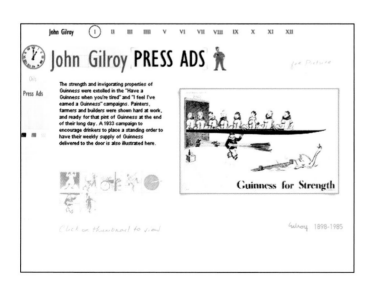

<most enduring> Webfactory continue their long-standing relationship with Guinness through the virtual "Gilroy Is Good For You" exhibition Web site. The site presents the versatility and prolific output of John Gilroy, creator of the famous Guinness Toucan, and some of the most enduring advertising images ever produced.

<fitting online environment> Taking the traditional poster design mark-up techniques used by Gilroy in his own work, fused with a newmedia approach to design, Webfactory created a fitting online environment to present John Gilroy's artistic talents.

<glimpse at the lifespan> Webfactory drew on one of Gilroy's most famous campaigns—"Guinness Time"— using the well-known clock face as the main navigational interface. Showing the progression of Gilroy's work in poster concepts,print ads and point-of-sale items, the Web site gives the viewer a glimpse at the lifespan of entire Gilroy concepts, even showing how Gilroy campaigns influenced modern Guinness advertising.

<themes and concepts> The site is divided into twelve sections: John Gilroy, Strength, Food, Doctors' Books, Circus & Zoo, Toucan, Sport, War Effort, Post Gilroy, Postcards, Exhibition and Book—each illustrating a range of advertising themes and concepts in which Gilroy and Guinness were involved.

</pageref>
<35><rhp>

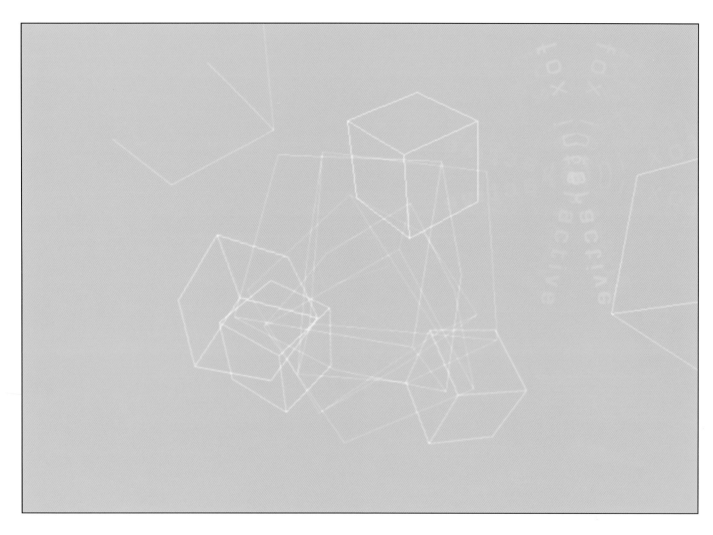

`<html>`
`<head>`

`<category>`	Promotional Advertising-CD-ROM`</head>`
`<award>`	Silver`</title>`
`<agency>`	Circumstance/Big Hand/San Francisco
`<client>`	Fox Interactive
`<art director>`	Brian Kralyevich
`<writer>`	Priscilla Bournonnais
`<digital artists>`	Lew Baldwin Fiel Valdez Brian Kralyevich
`<producer>`	Natalie Ammirato
`<multimedia>`	Circumstance
`<programmer>`	Sean Rooney
`<creative directors>`	Tim Barber David Bliss
`<hardware>`	Apple Macintosh PC
`<software>`	Adobe Illustrator, Adobe Photoshop Equilibrium Debabelizer, Macromedia Director

`</frameset>`
`<noframes>`
`<br><br>`
`</pageref>`
`<36><lhp>`
`<br><br>`

<the fickle attention>

Fox Interactive asked Circumstance to develop a digital press kit CD-ROM for the frenetic sensory overload that is the Electronic Entertainment Expo (E3). Giving Fox a public face that could engage the fickle attention of E3 goers and deliver information efficiently seemed impossible. Everyone retreated to the Zen center.

<hyperkinetic interface>

The eternal Tao bestowed a solution: a hyperkinetic interface and hypnotic techno soundtrack that form a no-nonsense system for journalists to easily download press releases and translate them into five languages on the fly.

<top-secret project>

But that's not all. With anticipation high for the upcoming release of its X-Files Game, Fox wanted a component of the press kit to amplify the excitement to fever pitch. Circumstance created a second CD-ROM that feeds conspiracy minded fans suggestions, hints, teasing glimpses of a dark, sinister world hiding a truth just beyond reach. Instead of a game demo, the CD was an intelligence report on the top secret project, using the show's inherent mystique—a closely guarded secret for immediate public release.

<award>
<Bronze>  </pic>

<html>
<head>

<category>	Promotional Advertising-CD-ROM</head>
<award>	Bronze</title>
<agency>	Reebok Interactive/Stoughton
<client>	Reebok Interactive
<art director>	Chuck Seelye
<writer>	Tony Gervino
<photographer>	Heater Advertising
<producer>	Marvin Chow
<multimedia>	Media Designs Brand Games Thrust Designs
<programmer>	Mike Taramykin
<hardware>	Apple Macintosh PC
<software>	C++

</frameset>
<noframes>

</pageref>
<38><lhp>

<a virtual tour>   The Reebok PULP CD-ROM was intended to give mass consumers a new-media vehicle to experience the Reebok Basketball Brand, its athletes, products and technologies. With a wide range of footwear and apparel, this interactive format takes the consumer on a virtual tour, giving athlete information and hookups, and behind the scenes looks.

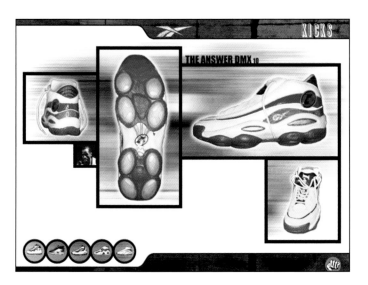

</pageref>
<39><rhp>

<award>
<Silver> </pic>

<html>
<head>

<category>	Promotional Advertising-Other Digital Advertising</head>
<award>	Silver</title>
<agency>	C3 Incorporated/New York
<client>	IBM
<digital artists>	Scott Williams Randall Hensley
<multimedia>	Think New Ideas
<programmers>	Marc Shifflet Carolyn Wagner
<creative director>	Randall Hensley
<hardware>	Apple Macintosh PC UNIX
<software>	Adobe Illustrator Adobe Photoshop Macromedia Director Macromedia Shockwave

</frameset>
<noframes>

</pageref>
<40><lhp>

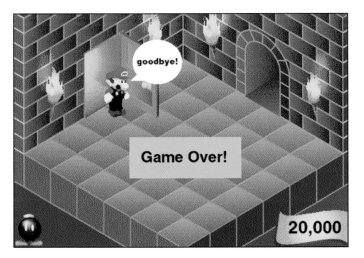

<64-bit technology> To interest prospects in AS/400 servers by promoting its 64-bit technology and Nintendo's use of it, C3 created a special game for the AS/400 Web site.

<arcade-quality action> The full, multidimensional game featured Nintendo's popular "Mario" character and incorporated many familiar aspects (such as rewards and foes) with almost arcade-quality action. A second phase of the game led players through a "qualification round" that enabled AS/400 to identify prospects and encourage them to learn more about Nintendo's applications on AS/400.

<thousands of winners> The highly successful game was supported with print mailings and online promotions. Thousands of winners received a Mario hat and opportunities to win Nintendo games and other prizes.

</pageref>
<41><rhp>

U.S. sending more ships to Gulf

Defense secretary's order comes as Clinton mulls possible military action against Iraq.

Inside

Nationline
Washington
World
Stocks
Scores
Baseball
NFL
NCAA
Books
Careers
Travel
Hot Sites
Web tech
Politics
Opinion

Winter-like storm pounds Plains

One dead, roads closed as wind, snow, rain wreak havoc.

MARKET REPORT
Reload for indexes

Dow	▼ 33.98 at	8863.98
Nasdaq	▲ 4.57 at	1865.62

TODAY'S BEST BETS

N C A A

The puck drops here!
Click here for breakaway

<html>
<head>

\<category\>	Promotional Advertising-Other Digital Advertising\</head\>
\<award\>	Bronze\</title\>
\<agency\>	Euro RSCG DSW Partners/Salt Lake City
\<client\>	Intel
\<url\>	www.dsw.com/oneshow/usatoday
\<art directors\>	Heather Brown Matt Davis
\<writers\>	Darren Vance Courtenay Martin
\<digital artist\>	Dallin Atkinson
\<producer\>	Jeff Bair
\<programmer\>	USA Today
\<creative director\>	Heather Brown
\<hardware\>	PC
\<software\>	Adobe Photoshop Gif Animator Text Editor Ulead PhotoImpact

</frameset>
<noframes>

</pageref>
42><lhp>

<homer's smarter brain> The goals were simple: push integration between traditional and new media, capitalize on the success of the Intel "Homer's Smarter Brain" TV spot, create Web-based advertising beyond an ordinary banner, sell Pentium® II processors and have fun.

<serious collaboration> Sounds easy, right? We had an idea. We had a willing client. We had Homer. We just didn't have much time. The inspiration to have Homer chase a doughnut through a live Web page came late in the campaign.

<pesky personalities> First problem? We had three days. Solution? Serious collaboration between DSW Partners, USA Today and various sources of caffeine. Problem two was convincing USA Today to let us mess around with the masthead. We answered that concern with outside-the-box thinking by our media folks, strong creative and our naturally pesky personalities. Third, we had three clients: Intel, USA Today and Fox. Each had to approve the creative and the execution. To solve this, we relied simply on liberal doses of pure grain alcohol.

<call to action> Early one morning in November 1998, millions of people accessed usatoday.com and saw Homer chase his beloved doughnut across the page. We're happy to report that tens of thousands followed the call to action to "Discover Intel's Greatest Challenge," and Homer eventually got his doughnut.

</pageref>
<43><rhp>

\<html\>
\<head\>

\<category\>	Corporate Image Consumer-Web Sites\</head\>
\<award\>	Gold\</title\>
\<agency\>	BBDO Interactive GmbH/Duesseldorf
\<client\>	Volkswagen AG
\<url\>	www.volkswagen-bora.de/
\<art directors\>	Michael Mittau Pepe Planas
\<writers\>	Udo Boehlefeld Oliver Guimarez
\<digital artist\>	Pepe Planas
\<producers\>	Marcus Paul Martin Grosseloser
\<programmer\>	Mick Baltes
\<creative director\>	Chris Bauer
\<hardware\>	Apple Macintosh PC
\<software\>	Adobe Photoshop Macromedia Flash

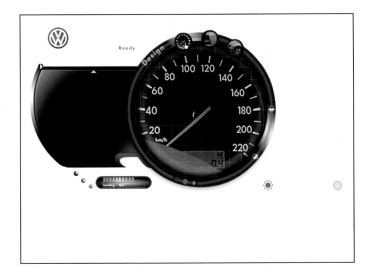

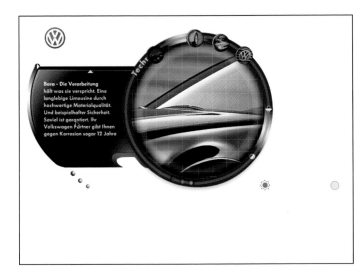

<awareness strategy> The Bora represents a very interesting product in a highly segmented market. Due to this segmentation, a coherent multimedia communication strategy was crucial for building awareness of the car.

<passion and fun> The Bora communicates passion and driving fun. This approach is visible on posters, TV commercials, billboards and print ads. The emotional dimension of the product is central to the strategy's overall style.

<conserve the style> From the outset of the planning process for the Bora Web site, we have endeavored to transfer the approach from classic media forms to interactive ones. Our principle goal has been to conserve the overall style while adding new means of interactivity and dialogue. Since the communication of a sporty and technological image is integral to the positioning of the Bora, we have opted to use a highly interactive and technological interface for the presentation of the product information.

<the ideal media> By incorporating visual elements and sounds which recall science fiction feature films, we have created an atmosphere that not only fits seamlessly into the general advertising approach but is also ideally suited to the Web and interactive media.

G-SHOCK

BABY-G

- Baby-G
- G-lide Street/Snow
- G-lide Surfing
- File
- Toughlabel

	ToughLabel	Baby-G	G-lide Surfing
Shock Resistant Housing	Shock Resistant Housing	Shock Resistant Housing	
100M Water Resistance	100M Water Resistance	200M Water Resistance	
12/24 Hour Formats	12/24 Hour Formats	12/24 Hour Formats	
Auto Calendar	Auto Calendar	Auto Calendar	
Hourly Time Signals	Hourly Time Signals	Hourly Time Signals	
	Countdown Alarm	Countdown Alarm	
	Daily Alarm	Daily Alarm	
	Multifunction Alarm		
1/100 Sec Stopwatch	1/100 Sec Stopwatch	1/100 Sec Stopwatch	
	Surfer/Dancer Animation		
E-L Backlight	E-L Backlight	E-L Backlight	
	Name Display		
3 Melodies and Beep Alarms			

<html>
<head>

<category>	Corporate Image Consumer-Web Sites</head>
<award>	Silver</title>
<agency>	Razorfish/New York
<client>	Casio/G-Shock
<url>	www.gshock.com
<art director>	David Warner
<writers>	Matt Hanlon Louis Zonis
<digital artists>	Sean Nassy Henry Min Leen Al-Bassam
<producer>	Louis Zonis
<programmers>	Shin Ogino Matt Hanlon Kevin Cancienne
<creative director>	Peter Seidler
<hardware>	Apple Macintosh PC
<software>	Adobe Illustrator Adobe Photoshop Macromedia Flash

</frameset>
</pageref> <noframes>
<lhp>

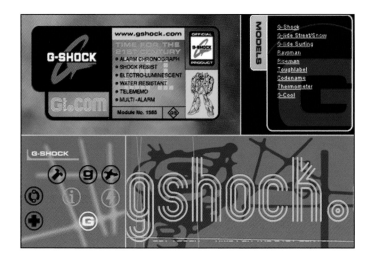

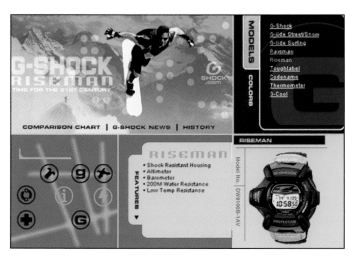

<the "G" stands> G-shock, the premier brand of Casio Timepieces, is a wristwatch with an attitude. The "G" stands for "gravity" and the "shock" represents the watch's resilience.

<fast-paced, dynamic> Casio felt the Web-based environment would best depict the fast-paced, dynamic attitude that G-Shock engenders. Also, aware of the ever-growing number of 15- to 30-year-old users. Casio knew the Web had the potential to reach a large number of G-shock's target consumers.

<with an attitude> Using bold, rich colors, extreme-sports visuals, vivid streetlife imagery and daring navigation, Razorfish created a presence with an attitude befitting G-shock. A unique six-frame layout provides fast-paced navigation through a site with constant movement and change. Users can download their own desktop G-Shock and explore a complete Baby-G and G-Shock catalog, including a Comparison Chart, a History feature and an Upcoming Watches section.

<embodying edgy spirit> As part of an integrated promotional campaign, the site also highlights upcoming Casio-sponsored extreme-sports events with video clips and images, provides an E-mail Us/information feature, a Retail Locator and a G-Shock Survival Stories section.

<with an attitude> Gshock.com creates a living hub for the G-Shock enthusiast whose lifestyle embodies the edgy spirit of the watch.

>

</pageref>
<47><rhp>

<html>
<head>

<category>	Corporate Image Consumer-Web Sites</head>
<award>	Bronze</title>
<agency>	DoubleYou/Barcelona
<client>	Seat España
<url>	toledo.seat.es/
<art director>	Blanca Piera
<writer>	Esther Pino
<digital artist>	Joakim Borgström Oriol Quin
<producer>	David Esteve
<programmers>	Joakim Borgström Imma Valls
<creative director>	Daniel Solana
<hardware>	Apple Macintosh, PC
<software>	Allaire Home Site, Adobe Illustrator Adobe Photoshop, Gif Builder Macromedia Fireworks, Ulead Gif Animator

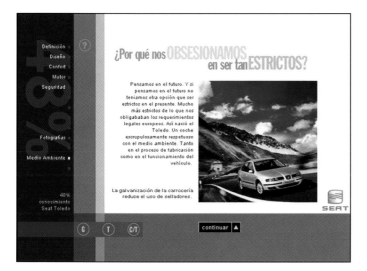

<original navigation> This Web site presents the new model for Seat through an original navigation system based on the knowledge of the car acquired by the user.

<optional answers> The interactive experience begins with the question, "Observe this front frontal and tell us what you think," with two choices as an answer. Following the chosen answer, the site moves on to a new page featuring certain characteristics of the car and three more optional answers in order to continue.

<by the user> This mode allows the visitor to advance through the site, covering up to twelve different pages that contain everything about the new model in the order of preference established by the user, depending on his choices.

<dynamic elements> Some of the pages have interesting interactive and dynamic elements, such as a crash test to assess the effectiveness of the airbags and an interactive photo album of the new model.

</pageref>
<49><rhp>

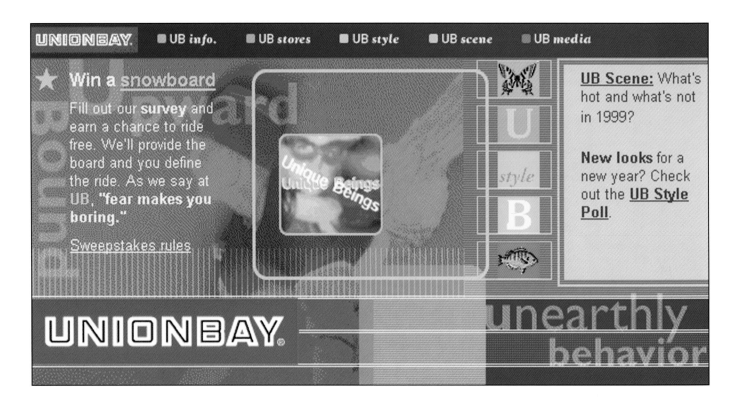

\<html\>
\<head\>

\<category\>	Corporate Image Consumer-Web Sites\</head\>
\<award\>	Bronze\</title\>
\<agency\>	Free Range Media/Seattle
\<client\>	Unionbay
\<url\>	www.unionbay.com
\<art director\>	Marion Hebert
\<writers\>	Simone Hodges Sarah Hilbert
\<digital artist\>	Corinne Broom
\<producers\>	Kimberly Andrews Patrick Cousans
\<multimedia\>	Michael Elliott
\<programmers\>	Patrick Kent Josh Bihary
\<creative directors\>	Cari Wade Kent Ord
\<hardware\>	PC

\</frameset\>
\<noframes\>
\<br\>\<br\>

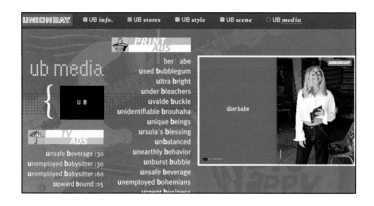

<much about
"lifestyle">

The Unionbay label is as much about "lifestyle" as it is about style. In creating unionbay.com, we tried to capture the energy and youth of the Unionbay teen. Focusing on the company's strategy of being an "American alternative" to today's youth, we developed an all-American site that complemented Unionbay's print and TV campaigns. Through the use of bright colors, playful type and compelling imagery, we created a site that reflects the attitude of today's teenagers and increases Unionbay's brand recognition.

<dedication to
serving>

Content on the site reaches out to the target group by appealing to their sense of "alternative" activities and interests. The UB Scene section uses the arenas of "extreme" sports and alternative music to promote Unionbay sponsored events, while reinforcing the company's dedication to serving the interests of American youth.

>

</pageref>
<51><rhp>

<html>
<head>

<category>	Corporate Image Consumer-Other Digital Advertising</head>
<award>	Gold</title>
<agency>	R/GA Interactive/New York
<client>	Discovery Communications
<writer>	John Rabasa
<digital artists>	Nathalie De La Gorce Sasha Kurtz Jeremy Lasky
<producer>	Scott Schneider
<programmer>	John Jones
<creative directors>	John Dire Frank Lantz
<hardware>	Apple Macintosh

</frameset>
<noframes>

</pageref>
<52><lhp>

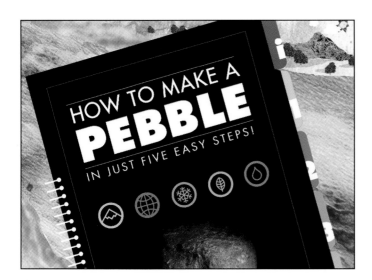

</pageref>
<53><rhp>

<award>
<Silver> </pic>

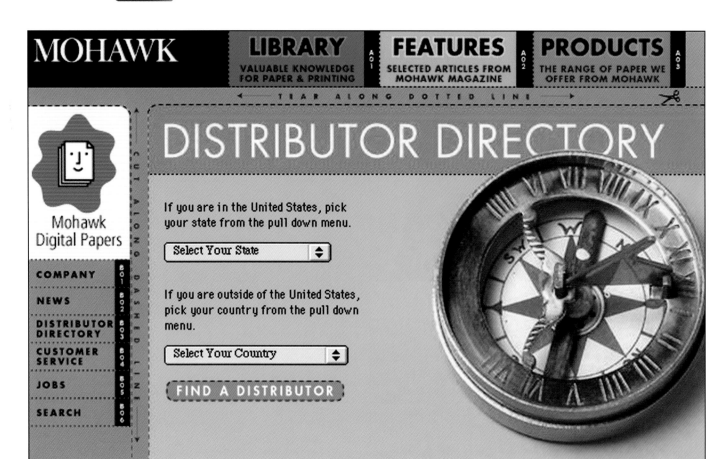

<html>
<head>

<category>	Corporate Image Business to Business-Web Sites</head>
<award>	Silver</title>
<agency>	ADJACENCY/San Francisco
<client>	Mohawk Paper Mills
<url>	www.mohawkpaper.com
<art directors>	Bernie DeChant Dave Le
<writer>	Laura Shore
<digital artist>	Dave Le
<photographer>	Seamus
<producers>	Jen Wolf Jen Sykes
<programmers>	Carlo Calica Matt Kirchstein Anton Prastowo
<creative director>	Bernie DeChant
<hardware>	Apple Macintosh
<software>	Adobe Photoshop Adobe Illustrator BBEdit

</frameset>
<noframes>

</pageref>
<54><lhp>

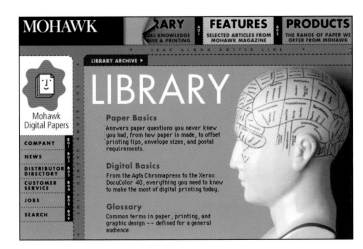

<old-fashioned way> For over one hundred years, Mohawk Paper Mills has sold paper the old-fashioned way, by putting it in the hands of designers and printers. Paper is tactile. You can pick it up, fold it, roll it into a ball... activities made cumbersome–if not impossible–once you introduce a computer monitor into the picture.

<the solution> We racked our brains over how to effectively showcase the subtleties of paper to the customer. We realized the solution was self-evident–make the site out of paper.

<the personalities> Fold-and-cut lines; objects laid on top of the site like paper weights; tear-off tabs (literally), etc. A photographer shot a series of objects, each one trying to convey through metaphor the personalities of each paper. Nuts and bolts for Opaque, the workhorse paper for everyday printing; an assortment of marbles for Options, a paper available in a wide array of colors and finishes.

<rocketed them> Adjacency's goal was to develop a site that print designers could appreciate on a visual and (virtually) tactile level while still providing all the information needed to choose the right paper. We took a 121-year-old company and rocketed them into the future of marketing.

</pageref>
<55><rhp>

<award>
<Bronze>  </pic>

<html>
<head>

<category>	Corporate Image Business to Business-Web Sites</head>
<award>	Bronze</title>
<agency>	SF Interactive/San Francisco
<client>	Moonstone Mountain Equipment
<url>	www.moonstone.com/
<art director>	Amy Franceschini
<digital artist>	Karl Jayne
<producers>	Lisa Herbert Michael Smethhurst
<multimedia>	SF Interactive
<programmers>	Cheryl Stephenson, Matt Brick Alejandro Levins, Michael Macrone
<creative director>	Bruce Carlisle
<hardware>	Apache PC
<software>	Adobe Photoshop, Allaire Homesite Claris Filemaker Pro Equilibrium Debabelizer, WebGen

</frameset>
</pageref>   <noframes>
<56><lhp>

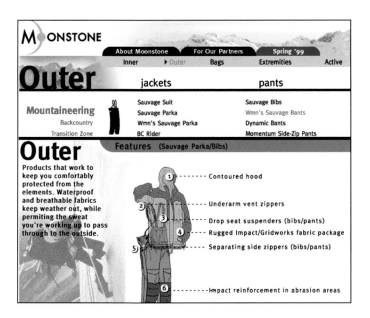

<opportunity to view>   The Moonstone Web site gives retailers, vendors, sales representatives and consumers the opportunity to view the wide range of Moonstone products and make purchasing decisions via an online medium. The site, designed primarily as a business-to-business site, was built as a tool to help re-position Moonstone as an innovator in the outdoor equipment industry.

<easily accessible>   Moonstone Mountain Equipment is a manufacturer of extreme-sports clothing targeted towards outdoor enthusiasts, specifically a younger generation of outdoor enthusiasts. Moonstone provides quality products and information for outdoor specialty retailers, people who know the outdoors and people who work in outdoor professions like ski and avalanche patrol, as well as wilderness rescue teams where outdoor equipment and easily accessible information are essential.

<real, simple, quality>   The design of the site is driven by its photography, which reflects the personality of Moonstone: real, simple, quality. The interface communicates the brand while providing access to extensive information about both the products, and how Moonstone does business.

<a variety>   Among the compelling features are an online workbook with product illustra-tions, a "For Our Partners" section, where Moonstone retailers can find information on sales incentive programs, e-mail Moonstone with questions and download a variety of Moonstone materials directly from the Web.

</pageref>
<57><rhp>

<award>
<Gold>  </pic>

<html>
<head>

<category>	Corporate Image Business to Business-CD-ROM</head>
<award>	Gold</title>
<agency>	Elephant Seven Multimedia GmbH/Hamburg
<client>	Daimler-Chrylser AG
<art director>	Sabine Grammersdorf
<writer>	Sven Mentel
<digital artist>	Madeleine Richter
<producer>	Ralf-Ingo Koch
<programmer>	Ralf-Ingo Koch
<creative directors>	Barbara Schmidt Paul Apostolou
<hardware>	Apple Macintosh PC
<software>	Macromedia Director, Media Composer QuickTime, QuickTime VR

</frameset>
<noframes>

</pageref>
<58><lhp>

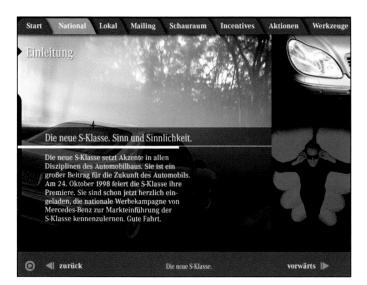

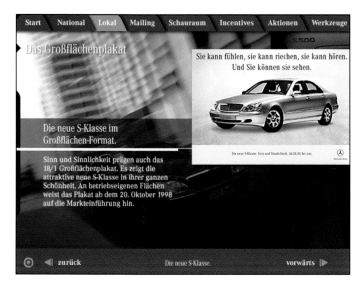

<communication tool> The Mercedes-Benz Partnerleitfaden on CD-ROM is an internal communication tool that informs about 800 Mercedes-Benz dealers in Germany of the marketing activities for the launch of new model ranges. The S-class Partnerleitfaden went out to the partners in September 1998.

<gain inspiration> Why a CD-ROM and not a conventional printed catalogue? Simple—the electronic version has distinct advantages: In QuickTime VR, dealers can move freely around two digitalized showrooms to get an impression of the showroom decoration materials available. Mercedes-Benz partners gain inspiration from examples of customer mailings which are available as data files. They can also choose from a wide selection of incentives, giveaways and request these immediately by order form. Partners are, of course, also informed of Mercedes-Benz print, radio, TV and outdoor advertising, allowing film and radio commercials to be presented as they are intended: in sound and pictures.

<step up a gear> Even the partners' own advertising activities have stepped up a gear: special tools allow dealers to edit pre-designed ad motifs on a PC. This saves a lot of work, as well as time and money.

>

</pageref>
<59><rhp>

WELCOME

HOW IT WORKS

CONTENTS

QUIT

<html>
<head>

<category>	Corporate Image Business to Business-CD-ROM</head>
<award>	Silver</title>
<agency>	Duffy Design/Minneapolis
<client>	FIFA 1999 Women's World Cup
<art director>	Alan Colvin
<writers>	Chuck Carlson Robin Meredith Alan Colvin
<digital artist>	Cindy Bennett
<producer>	Mark Sandau
<multimedia>	Mark Sandau Leslie Fandrich
<programmers>	Mark Sandau Leslie Fandrich
<hardware>	Apple Macintosh
<software>	Adobe AfterEffects, Adobe Photoshop Adobe Illustrator, Macromedia Director

</frameset>
<noframes>

</pageref>
<60><lhp>

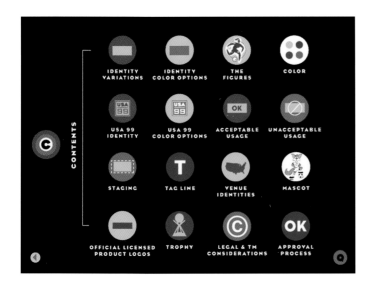

<destined for greatness>

This CD-ROM is designed to provide artwork and guidelines for the 1999 FIFA Women's World Cup Identity System. The foundation of the 1999 Women's World Cup as a brand is being laid; use of the identity according to these standards will assure that the brand being built is destined for greatness. To achieve this goal, all communications surrounding the event must be of the highest caliber.

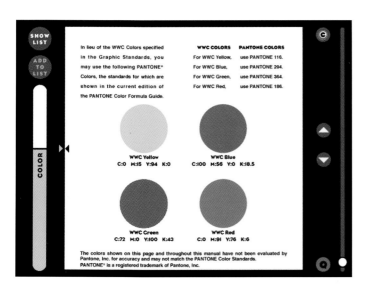

</pageref>

<61><rhp>

the **NETWORK** that
ENTERTAINS
the **WORLD**

→ **Vibrant brand**

→ **More subscribers**

→ **Young, dynamic audience**

→ **Original programming**

the network

\<html\>
\<head\>

\<category\>	Corporate Image Business to Business-Other Digital Advertising\</head\>
\<award\>	Silver\</title\>
\<agency\>	Genex Interactive/Los Angeles
\<client\>	E! Entertainment Television
\<art director\>	Jason Drake
\<digital artist\>	Jason Drake
\<producer\>	Ray Odell
\<programmer\>	Thomas Deaton
\<creative director\>	David Glaze
\<hardware\>	Apple Macintosh
\<software\>	Adobe AfterEffects
	Adobe Illustrator
	Adobe Photoshop
	Macromedia Freehand
	Macromedia SoundEdit
	Media 100
	MTropolis
	Quicktime

\</frameset\>
\</pageref\>   \<noframes\>
62\>\<lhp\>   \<br\>\<br\>
\<br\>\<br\>

<storytelling> The sales force at E! Entertainment Television needed a presentation that was as sexy and trendy as their highly visible brand. Genex Interactive developed an E! Entertainment Sales Presentation CD-ROM that tells the story of the brand, shows, audience demographics and program schedule, while showcasing the attitude and style of the trademark on-air personalities. For the first time, sales reps could easily show bumpers, statistical audience information and clips, giving a true representation of the E! Entertainment brand personality.

<flexibility> High energy music and video sets the tone, then a flexible navigation enables the sales team to customize the presentation to the interests of the audience. Genex Interactive also added a five-minute E! video to the CD-ROM. The E! sales force was trained to run the CD utilizing laptop computers and data projectors, which maximize the CD's impact.

</pageref>
<63><rhp>

<award>
<Gold> </pic>

<html>
<head>

<category>	Direct Marketing-Web Sites</head>
<award>	Gold</title>
<agency>	Sapient/Studio Archetype/San Francisco
<client>	E-Trade
<url>	www.etrade.com
<art director>	Art Kilinski
<digital artists>	Jimmy Chen, Angela Hum Paula Meiselman, Henrik Olsen
<producers>	Bradley Allen, Alison Brush Caroll Lee, Linda Lee, Jason Widmann
<multimedia>	Bryan Wu Eric Shank
<programmers>	Rick Lehrer, Chris Jones
<creative directors>	Mark Crumpacker, Sam Fuetsch Lillian Svek
<hardware>	Apple Macintosh
<software>	Adobe Illustrator, Adobe Photoshop

</frame-
</pageref>   set>
<noframes>

\<time-crunched but agile\> E*TRADE pioneered online investing services in 1992. Today, with nearly 70 places on the Internet to buy and sell stock, E-trade remains the leader; it's a compelling destination with a community of financially attuned, time-crunched but agile computer users who have found one place on the Web for all things financial.

\<making a pleasure\> E*TRADE came to Studio Archetype to lead the redesign. It turns first time visitors into account holders makes doing business fast and easy, and assures security and privacy. E*Trade's design encompasses branding, content, user tools, ease of use and the ineffable fun factor—making a pleasure out of online investing and related tasks.

\<heavyweight\> Like a growing number of heavyweight transactional and commerce destinations, E*TRADE's Web site leans more toward a software application than a home page. The interface design provides branding and navigation and also empowers users to quickly and easily perform tasks. Customers expect it to be easy to tune the site's resources toward their own vital interests.

\<then we crafted\> Through user research and extensive collaboration with E*TRADE's product and technology staff, Studio Archetype helped the company refine its site strategy and architecture. Then we crafted a new interface for E*TRADE's Web presence.

\<br\>

<award>
<Silver>  </pic>

<html>
<head>

<category>	Direct Marketing-Web Sites</head>
<award>	Silver</title>
<agency>	USWeb/CKS/Sausalito
<client>	Levi Strauss and Co.
<url>	store.us.dockers.com:80/store/home.asp
<art director>	Tim Kain
<writer>	Mary Jeanne Deery
<digital artists>	Hollimarie O'Carroll, Joey Wu
<photographers>	Stewart Ferebee, David Martinez, Richard Rethemeyer
<producers>	AnneLise Staal, Traci Cassell, Charl Morkel
<multimedia>	USWeb/CKS
<programmers>	Judi Hengeveld, Aaron Franklin
<creative director>	Mark Frankel
<hardware>	Apple Macintosh
<software>	Adobe AfterEffects, Adobe Illustrator Adobe ImageReady, Adobe Photoshop Equilibrium Debabilizer, Macromedia Fireworks

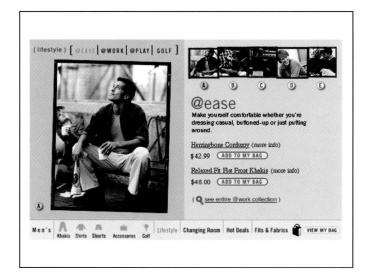

<a consultative experience>

In 1998, Levi Strauss and Co. decided to sell their Dockers Khakis directly to consumers. USWeb/CKS's goal was to create a shopping experience that would expand the Dockers Khakis brand target to a younger audience. The entire site serves as a style consultant for today's new combined casual look for work, play and ease. Throughout the conception and design of the Dockers Khakis site, we strove to create an energized environment wrapped around a consultative experience.

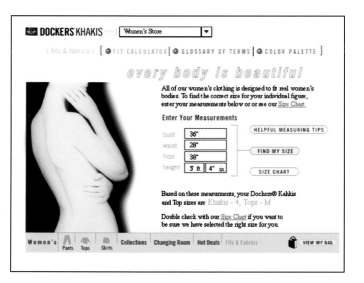

</pageref>
<67><rhp>

<html>
<head>

<category>	Direct Marketing-Web Sites</head>
<award>	Bronze</title>
<agency>	USWeb/CKS/Sausalito
<client>	Levi Strauss and Co.
<url>	store.us.levi.com/store/home.asp
<art director>	Colleen Stokes
<writer>	Lauren Kerr
<digital artists>	Matt Browne Kim Nations
<photographer>	David Peterson
<producer>	Michele Jacobs
<multimedia>	USWeb/CKS
<programmer>	Kevin Fox
<creative director>	Michael Borosky
<hardware>	Apple Macintosh
<software>	Adobe Illustrator Adobe ImageReady Adobe Photoshop

</frameset>
<noframes>
</pageref>

<lhp>

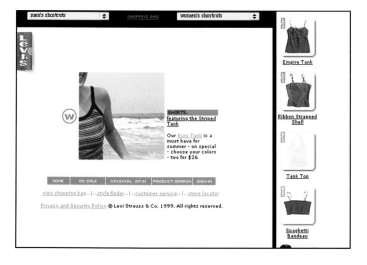

<make it simple>

Levi's® Online Store was designed to be a fun, hip shopping experience that responds creatively to diverse styles and tastes. The new Levi's® site launched offering a broad selection of Levi's® apparel and accessories for men and women, including a wide selection of SilverTab® brand clothing and other hard-to-find items. Easy navigation, multiple product views and the ability to see the clothing up close make it simple for consumers to find and purchase the styles they want.

<about their taste>

The site was designed to appeal to the youthful consumer while welcoming all loyal Levi's® jeans enthusiasts. Exciting interactive features, such as the Style Finder, help shoppers locate the products that fit their personal style when they answer a series of fun questions about their taste in music, clothing and leisure activities.

<html>
<head>

<category>	Integrated Branding Campaign</head>
<award>	Gold</title>
<agency>	Euro RSCG DSW Partners/Salt Lake City
<client>	Intel
<url>	www.dsw.com/oneshow/homer
<hardware>	PC
<software>	Adobe ImageReady Adobe PhotoShop Ulead GifAnimator

</frameset>
<noframes>

</pageref>
<70><lhp>

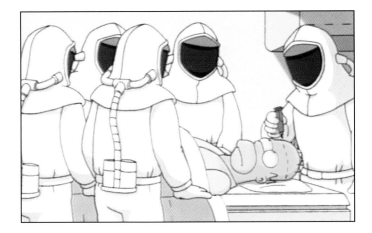

<the before and after> Homer Simpson, Ph.D. A contradiction in terms? Perhaps, but if there's a more famously incapable brain to illustrate the before and after of owning a Pentium®II processor, we couldn't find it.

<re-education> Through the usual torturous research, we found consumers needed re-education on the role of Intel® processors. So we animated the Intel® BunnyPeople™ characters, bribed Homer with a dough-nut-and-sprinkles, and gave him a smarter brain courtesy of a Pentium®II processor. This became one of the most popular Intel® TV spots ever.

<"ummm... doughnuts."> With the push to integrate across all media, enter Marge, Bart, Lisa and the gang with "Homer's Holiday Helper," an interactive Web page. There, both a pre- and post-operative Homer offered ideas for the "Bart" or "Lisa" on your gift list. The normal Homer's thoughts? "Ummm... doughnuts." The smarter Homer's? Tons of ideas to beef up a PC. People accessed this page via Intel.com, banners and unique sponsorships where the characters interacted with live Web pages.

<seamless experience> In the end, we had a seamless experience between traditional and new media. Plus, we worked with some of the most creative people on the planet (Fox) and with a character who has truly influenced all of us. Doh!

>

</pageref>
<71><rhp>

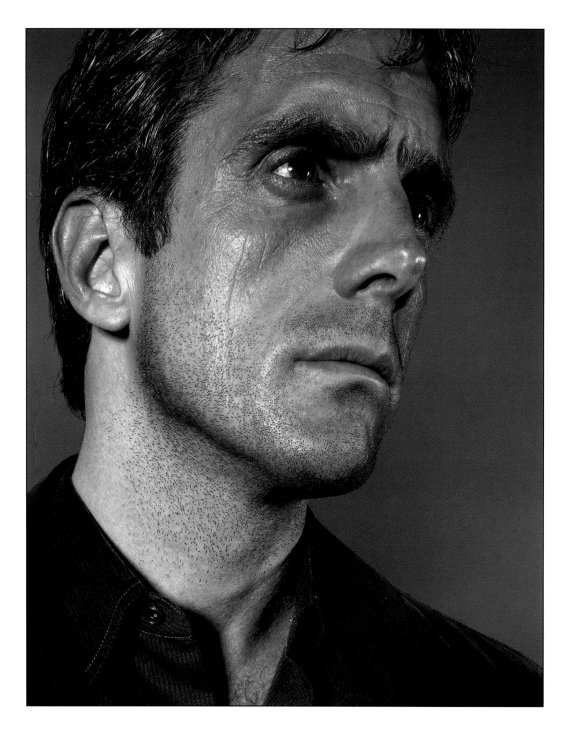
<html>
<head>

<category>	Integrated Branding Campaign</head>
<award>	Silver</title>
<agency>	Wieden & Kennedy/Portland
<client>	Calvin Klein
<url>	www.wk.com/newbiz/ck_ss.htm
	(username:brit98.password:pr1nc55)

</frameset>
<noframes>

</pageref>

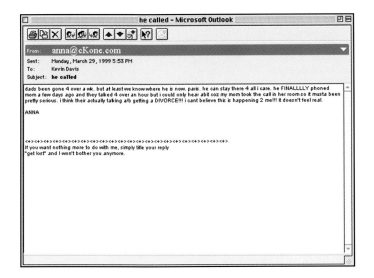

<to reconnect> Wieden & Kennedy combined the Calvin Klein aesthetic and cK one's positioning with this generation's "societal/consumer trend," communications' technology. This combination was established to reconnect the cK one brand with its consumers.

<of the present> Although these worlds are very different, they are both worlds of the present, of today. We have created a campaign comprised of ten characters. Each with his/her own life, each with his/her own e-mail address, but all connected. When consumers send them an e-mail, they will respond with a series of messages that will take the consumers into an unfolding drama. Always current, modern and of today.

</pageref>
<73><rhp>

<html>
<head>

<category>	Integrated Branding Campaign</head>
<award>	Bronze</title>
<agency>	Ogilvy Interactive
<client>	IBM
<url>	www.oandmi.com/media/eculture/work/showcase/html (username: media, password: banners)
<art director>	Warren Kemp
<writer>	David Levy
<digital artist>	Rachael Heapps
<producers>	Jude Raymond Fish Kate Kehoe
<programmer>	David Carson/Compound
<creative director>	Jan Leth
<hardware>	Apple Macintosh
<software>	Adobe Illustrator Adobe Photoshop Enliven Macromedia Director Macromedia Flash

</frameset>
<noframes>

</pageref>
<74><lhp>

<energize> Our goal with this campaign was to show how IBM e-business solutions have helped a range of companies, large and small, energize their businesses by taking advantage of the Internet. Internally, the campaign was dubbed "e-culture"— because the broader intention was to tout how Internet-based solutions (with IBM, of course, boldly leading the way) have pervaded countless aspects of contemporary life—whether you're making an airline reservation on the Web, or hiking through the wilderness in boots you bought from an online store.

<unique stories> Each company profiled in the campaign had its own unique e-business solution (combos of IBM hardware, software, design and consulting services), so it was important that each story—though unmistakably IBM—had a feel of its own. And since e-business is all about pushing the electronic envelope, so to speak, it was necessary to do the same with this campaign—by developing intriguing interactivity for the Enliven banners, and whizzy RealFlash "mini-spots" for the pop-up interstitials.

<show the way> The interactive banners work, one hopes, by offering a bit of fun before the serious sell. Because there's no way to fully explain any IBM-customer relationship in a banner space, we created a series of interactive visual metaphors. One example: for REI, a retailer of outdoor gear, the cursor becomes a "flashlight" which helps the user search for a camp-site; and the copy talks about helping your business "find its way to the Web."

<integrated imagery> As for the overall look, it was important to integrate the imagery used in the print work, as well as the essence of each company helped by IBM. So the banners follow the lead of the IBM print and broadcast work—very monochromatic so the red 'e' jumps out at you. For the testimonial pop-ups, key colors were extracted from each customer's Web site to create individual palettes. We really wanted to keep these pop-ups free of clutter—to give the imagery as much breathing room as possible without overwhelming the top-line message or the deeper levels of content in the case studies.

>

</pageref>
<75><rhp>

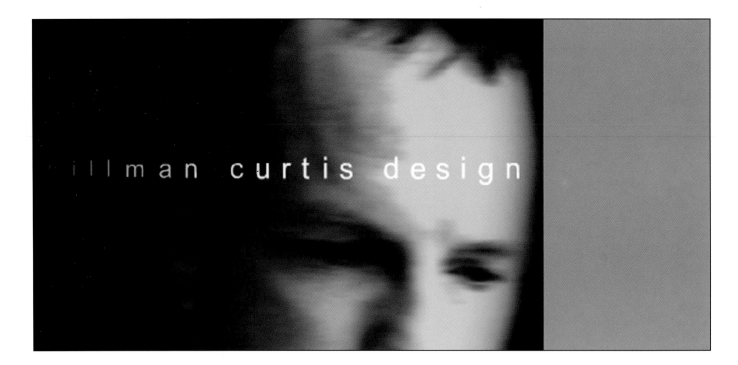

\<html>
\<head>

\<category>	Self-Promotion-Web Sites\</head>
\<award>	Gold\</title>
\<agency>	hillmancurtis.com/New York
\<client>	hillmancurtis.com
\<url>	www.hillmancurtis.com/
\<art director>	Hillman Curtis
\<writers>	Hillman Curtis Christina Manning Curtis
\<digital artists>	Hillman Curtis Michael Davis
\<photographers>	Jeff Wong Hillman Curtis David Hartt
\<producer>	Hillman Curtis
\<multimedia>	Hillman Curtis
\<programmer>	Hillman Curtis
\<creative director>	Hillman Curtis
\<hardware>	Apple Macintosh PC
\<software>	Adobe AfterEffects Adobe Photoshop Adobe Premier Macromedia Dreamweaver Macromedia Fireworks Macromedia Flash Macromedia Freehand Macromedia Soundedit

\</frameset>
\<noframes>
\
\

\</pageref>
\
\

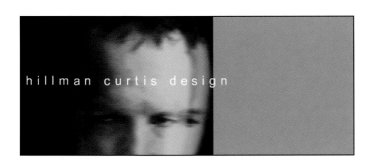

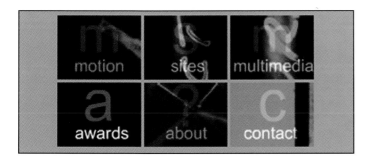

<an epiphany-like rush>

My commitment to motion graphics came to me in an epiphany-like rush. I was in the audience at a design conference, and Kyle Cooper was presenting his work, conveying his passion for the medium of motion graphic design. As he demonstrated the title sequence for Donnie Brasco, I recognized that I had long harbored an interest in motion graphics.

<a minimalist and intuitive navigational structure>

The hillmancurtis.com site was designed to reflect this commitment to motion graphic design, specifically, motion graphic design for the Web. The opening spot was inspired by the Donnie Brasco film title, as well as by artist Bill Viola's work. I wanted the spot to be visually striking in terms of its imagery, its rhythm and its fluidity. In addition, it was crucial that the site be functional... that it work perfectly on 28.8 and above. Further, I wanted to present a minimalist and intuitive navigational structure, and give compelling examples of motion graphics.

<the power of motion>

The site is essentially a portfolio, a showcase of my commercial design–what we do is motion-based advertising. But for me, it is more than just the artistic medium that holds the site together. That is, I believe in the power of motion graphic design as a means to communicate in a distinctive, emotive way.

>

</pageref>
<77><rhp>

<award>
<Silver>  </pic>

MONKEYmedia™

interface design
information architecture
interaction technology

loading...

611 South Congress Avenue, Suite 310 • Austin, Texas 78704 • (512) 440-8000, 440-1050 fax • © 1998 MONKEYmedia, Inc.

<html>
<head>

<category>	Self-Promotion-Web Sites</head>
<award>	Silver</title>
<agency>	MONKEYmedia/Austin
<client>	New Media Industry
<url>	www.monkey.com/
<art directors>	Janna Buckmaster Eric J. Gould
<writers>	Eric J. Gould Janna Buckmaster
<multimedia>	Paulas W. Trisnadi Alice May Clark, David Richard Donald McCaskill, Arie Stavchansky Gerry Bassermann/Opus Nine
<hardware>	Apple Macintosh,PC
<software>	Adobe Illustrator, Adobe ImageReady Adobe Photoshop, Macromedia Dreamweaver, Macromedia Flash Macromedia SoundEdit, Quicktime

</frameset>
</pageref>   <noframes>
<78><lhp>

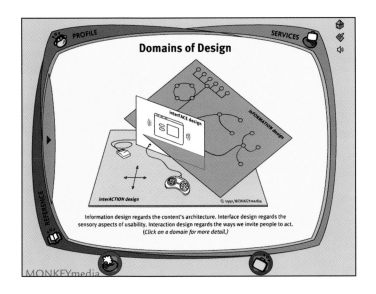

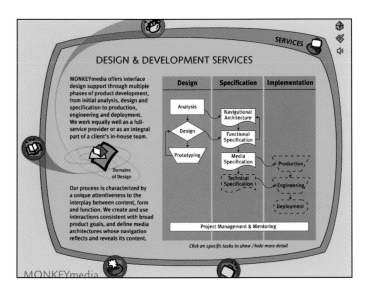

<consistent expertise> MONKEYmedia is a design and development firm specializing in interaction as a communications medium. They offer interface design, information architecture and interaction specification services as well as a diverse portfolio of intellectual properties for licensing. Unique in providing the desktop computing, new media and consumer electronics industries a design and technology resource focused specifically on human-computer interaction, they offer consistent expertise in maximizing product usability and audience participation.

<taste of the future> MONKEYmedia's new site includes interface design reference materials and examples of their cutting-edge intellectual properties. The ultra-sensory Flash version gives a taste of the future of the Web through pseudo-fisheye navigation techniques, fun vector animation and a beautifully textured audioscape. It not only showcases their portfolio, but also kinesthetically engages visitors with an exciting interface, and backs it all up with authoritative reference materials that can help all designers and developers make better products. Universal access is also available for disabled and mobile visitors.

</pageref>
<79><rhp>

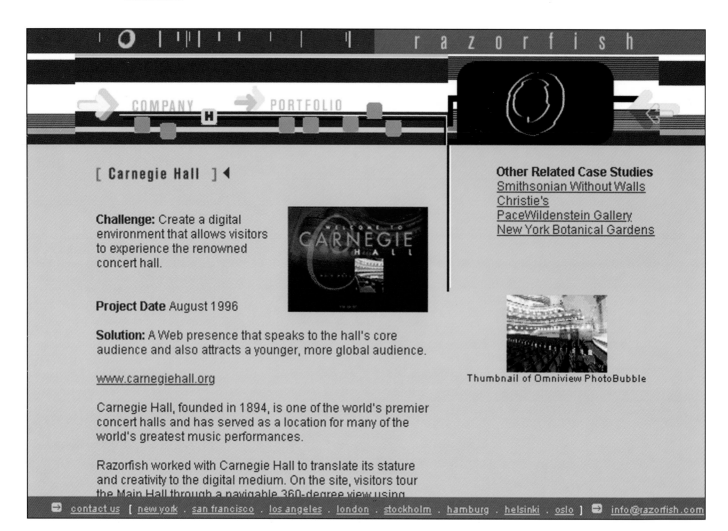

[Carnegie Hall] ◀

Challenge: Create a digital environment that allows visitors to experience the renowned concert hall.

Project Date August 1996

Solution: A Web presence that speaks to the hall's core audience and also attracts a younger, more global audience.

www.carnegiehall.org

Carnegie Hall, founded in 1894, is one of the world's premier concert halls and has served as a location for many of the world's greatest music performances.

Razorfish worked with Carnegie Hall to translate its stature and creativity to the digital medium. On the site, visitors tour the Main Hall through a navigable 360-degree view using

Other Related Case Studies
Smithsonian Without Walls
Christie's
PaceWildenstein Gallery
New York Botanical Gardens

Thumbnail of Omniview PhotoBubble

contact us [new york . san francisco . los angeles . london . stockholm . hamburg . helsinki . oslo] info@razorfish.com

<html>
<head>

<category>	Self-Promotion-Web Sites</head>
<award>	Bronze</title>
<agency>	Razorfish/New York
<client>	Razorfish
<url>	www.razorfish.com/
<art director>	Thomas Mueller
<digital artist>	Thomas Mueller
<producer>	Brandi Gil
<multimedia>	Jason Jeffries
<programmer>	Aaron Berkson
<creative director>	Thomas Mueller
<hardware>	Apple Macintosh PC
<software>	Adobe Illustrator Adobe Photoshop

</frameset>
<noframes>

</pageref>
<80><lhp>

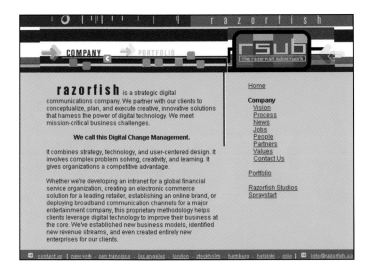

<identity>   Challenge: Be the brand. Solution: A site that embodies the Razorfish identity.

<needing to manage>   Razorfish is a strategic digital communications company. The company partners with clients to conceive, plan and execute leading edge solutions for organizations needing to manage digital change.

<flexible web presence>   Over the past year Razorfish has grown into a global firm with more than 400 individuals. The company needed a flexible Web presence that embodied the global Razorfish brand, showcased the scope of its Digital Change Management[sm] service offerings, presented company information and highlighted its extensive client base.

<six languages>   Razorfish.com reflects a unified brand and reinforces the distinct cultural identities of the company's eight offices. Published in six languages, English, UK English, German, Finnish, Swedish and Norwegian, the localized versions allow each office to tailor information to its target audience.

<a global team>   The site is template-based and dynamically published using Cold Fusion and an Oracle database. It features DHTML 4.0 and a verity search engine. Site content is managed via a dynamic content management system with workflow and foreign language support, allowing a global team of people to keep the content current and up-to-date.

</pageref>
<81><rhp>

<award>
<Gold>  </pic>

<html>
<head>

<category>	Self-Promotion-CD-ROM</head>
<award>	Gold</title>
<agency>	Red Sky Interactive/San Francisco
<client>	Red Sky Interactive
<art directors>	Clay Jensen, Genevieve Moore, Rob Brown
<writer>	Richard Ciccarone
<digital artists>	Michael Kosacki, Renaud Ternynck, Ken Cope Christina Neville, Jeff Essex
<producers>	Deirdre McGlashan, Amy Lee
<multimedia>	Red Sky Interactive
<programmers>	Marc Blanchard, Krister Olsson, Jade Zabrowski Irv Kalb, Sophie Jasson-Holt, Jeff Miller
<creative director>	Joel Hladacek
<hardware>	Apple Macintosh, PC
<software>	Adobe AfterEffects, Adobe Photoshop, Equilibrium Debabelizer, Macromedia Director, Maxon Cinema 4D

</frameset>
<noframes>
</pageref>

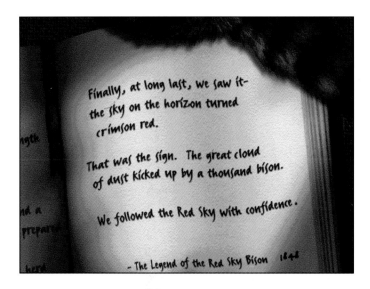

<a challenge> Every year Red Sky Interactive creates a demo CD-ROM, not only to showcase client work, but also to challenge the way the industry thinks about designing for the interactive medium. Their 1998 demo, "Red Sky on the Frontier" is no exception. With an eye decidedly towards the inevitable popularizing of broadband technologies, Red Sky proposes a very different view of the commercial, online presence. Styled in the spirit of the American movie westerns of the '30s and '40s, this live-action, anachronistic experience is both richly conceived and surprising in its interactivity. Join Red Sky's singing cowboy Gus Gilroy to catch a glimpse of what the Web may look like two years from now.

</pageref>
<83><rhp>

\<html>
\<head>

\<category>	Self-Promotion-CD-ROM\</head>
\<award>	Silver\</title>
\<agency>	Duffy Design/Minneapolis
\<client>	Fallon McElligott
\<art director>	Tom Riddle
\<multimedia>	Mark Sandau Leslie Fandrich
\<hardware>	Apple Macintosh
\<software>	Adobe AfterEffects Adobe Illustrator Adobe Photoshop Macromedia Director Macromedia SoundEdit 16

\</frameset>
\<noframes>
\
\

<we were silent> Fallon McElligott is a company that specializes in communicating–whether it's a brillant ad, a breakthrough consumer insight or a new branding campaign for one of our bluechip client partners. Talking about our clients, and talking to consumers, comes naturally. But when it comes to talking about ourselves, we were silent until this year.

<a virtual walk-through> The Fallon McElligott CD-ROM Press Kit allows us to talk about ourselves to a worldwide media audience (there is a US and int'l version). The kit, contained in a metal, tabbed binder (allowing for updates) contains facts and figures, client lists, historical highlights, biographies, photos, a CD-ROM and a reel of television spots (both VHS and PAL versions). The kit provides a virtual walk-through of the agency, giving viewers an inside glimpse into this unique organization where the work comes first and our clients are our friends.

>

</pageref>
<85><rhp>

Season's Greetings

>

<html>
<head>

<category>	Self-Promotion-Other Digital Advertising</head>
<award>	Gold</title>
<agency>	Nicholson NY/New York
<client>	Nicholson NY
<url>	www.nny.com/holiday
<art director>	Kevin Chiu
<digital artist>	Mayumi Sato
<programmer>	Wells Packard
<creative directors>	Kevin Chiu Tom Nicholson
<hardware>	Apple Macintosh
<software>	Adobe Photoshop Equilibrium Debabilizer Macromedia Director Macromedia Sound Edit Maya

</frameset>
<noframes>

</pageref>
<86><lhp>

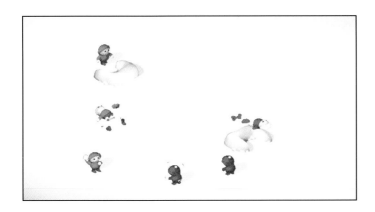

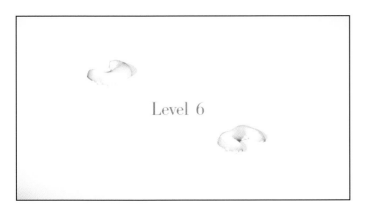

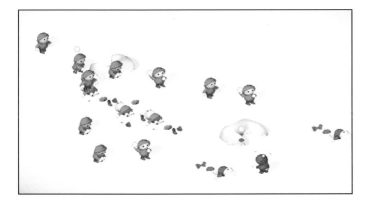

<combined spoof> SnowCraft was created as an interactive holiday greeting card for Nicholson NY's clients, friends and colleagues. Its objective was to promote awareness of the agency and to show off its creative, as well as its strategic and technological expertise. The game's designer envisioned a combined spoof of the 3-D orthographic game WarCraft and the two-dimensional snowball fight game the agency had developed for its 1997 holiday card.

<all of the positions> While the creative director designed key screens and character sketches, the agency's interaction designer began programming a game engine to control characters ability to toss objects and detect collisions. Using the original art as a starting point, the interaction designer fleshed out the in-between steps needed to animate character behaviors, added sound effects and then the team fine-tuned the interaction. The characters were then re-created in 3-D and all of the positions and angles necessary for the game were rendered. After alpha testing, 10 levels were added, including a bonus round round-winning payoff.

<attention and visits> The results were better than expected. After the enormous influx of holiday traffic subsided, Snowcraft continues to attract attention and visits to the agency's home page have increased by 600%.

>

</pageref>
<87><rhp>

\<html\>
\<head\>

\<category\>	Self-Promotion-Other Digital Advertising\</head\>
\<award\>	Silver\</title\>
\<agency\>	Hill Holliday Interactive/Boston
\<client\>	Hill Holliday Interactive
\<art directors\>	Murat Bodor Rob Mucciaccio
\<writer\>	Vashti Brotherhood
\<programmer\>	Jonathan Hurwitz
\<hardware\>	Apple Macintosh
\<software\>	Adobe Illustrator Adobe Photoshop Equilibrium Debabelizer GifBuilder Lotus Avian Streaming Media Lotus Domino Lotus Notes

\</frameset\>
\<noframes\>
\<br\>\<br\>

<without much thought>

In all honesty we had the wind at our backs on this one. The visual content supplied by the general advertising teams was inspirational design-wise. The words came quickly and without much thought. And no one was watching us. We just did what we felt was right and posted it. How often does that happen?

</pageref>
<89><rhp>

<award>
<Gold>   </pic>

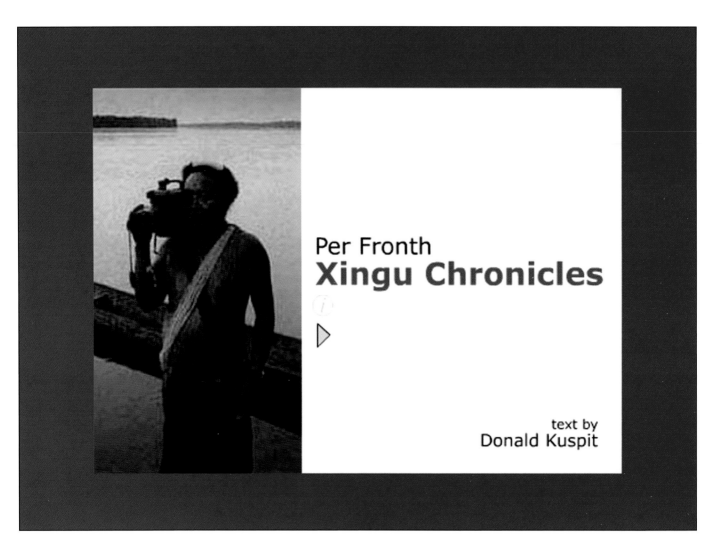

<html>
<head>

<category>	Non-Profit Organizations-Web Sites</head>
<award>	Gold</title>
<agency>	Blue Hypermedia/New York
<client>	Per Fronth/Rainforest Foundation
<url>	www.fronth.com
<art director>	James Roven
<writer>	Donald Kuspit
<digital artist>	James Roven
<hardware>	PC
<software>	Adobe Photoshop Macromedia Flash

</frameset>
<noframes>

</pageref>
<90><lhp>

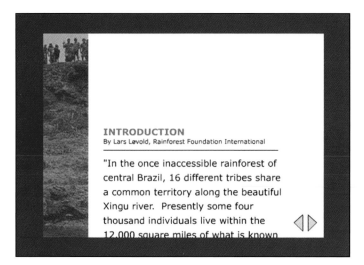

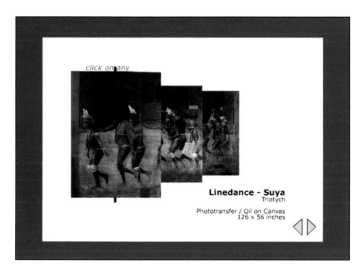

<the cause> The Xingu Chronicles site was created for the Rainforest Foundation International as part of a fundraising event to save the rainforests and peoples of the Xingu region of Brazil. This site uses streaming media to showcase the work of Norwegian artist Per Fronth, whose pieces chronicle the lives and culture of the Xingu natives. Proceeds from the sale of the artwork were donated to help the cause.

<the showcase> One of the challenges in showcasing artwork is to present it in a setting that augments, but doesn't compete with, the images. Well-known art critic Donald Kuspit prepared beautiful copy to accompany the presentation and we created a system of "pull-downs" for his text alongside each piece. With this system, there was no detracting from the initial presentation of each image.

Another challenge was to allow the audience the opportunity to get "close" to the images – enabling them to see texture and detail. In the case of the triptych piece, we created an intuitive "zoom" interface which brings each of the three panels into closer view.

<the feel> The end result is a site that fluidly combines text with Fronth's beautiful work in an environment that feels natural and non-invasive.

>

</pageref>
<91><rhp>

<award>
<Silver> </pic>

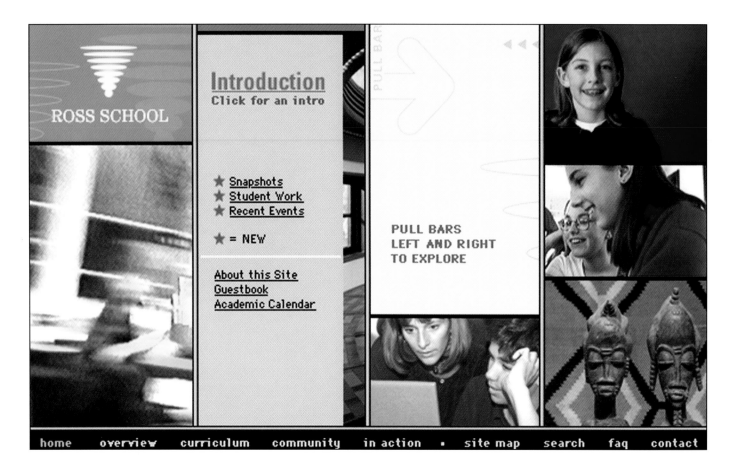

<html>
<head>

<category>	Non-Profit Organizations-Web Sites</head>
<award>	Silver</title>
<agency>	R/GA Interactive/New York
<client>	Ross School
<url>	www.ross.org/
<art director>	John DiRe
<digital artist>	John Rabasa
<producers>	Rachel Chou
	Robert Michaels
<programmer>	Greg Glass
<creative director>	Frank Lantz
<hardware>	PC
<software>	Macromedia Flash
	Microsoft Windows NT
	Information Server
	IPIX
	Interactive Pictures
	Real Audio & Video

</frameset>
<noframes>

<finally, school life>

Consistent navigation, useful features and goal-oriented design are all part of the thinking that went into the Ross School Web site's interaction design. Based on our identification of the most likely visitors we created four critical paths: the overview track provides an 'executive summary' of what makes the Ross School such a unique learning environment; the curriculum track presents an in-depth, cross-referenced look at the school's curriculum and examples of student work; the community section provides information about members of the Ross community, admissions and job openings; and, finally, "school life" gives visitors access to student-created Web sites and snapshots of life at the school throughout the year.

<the layer underneath>

Visual design for the Ross School Web site reflects the school's spirit of exploration and discovery, its diverse community, and its grounding in nature. The design we arrived at makes use of a rich palette of complex, earthy colors. It is modular and playful, with pages breaking down into sections that slide like shoji screens. Visitors are invited to jump in and experience it by pulling on the panels and uncovering the layer underneath. The site, like the school, emphasizes delight in learning.

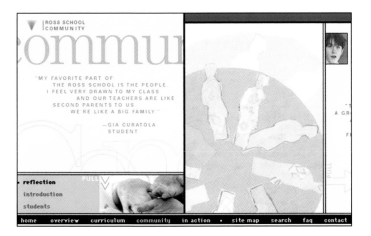

</pageref>
<93><rhp>

<award>
<Bronze>  </pic>

<html>
<head>

<category>	Non-Profit Organizations-Web Sites</head>
<award>	Bronze</title>
<agency>	NKH&W/Kansas City
<client>	Kansas City Ad Club
<url>	www.kcadclub.org/
<art director>	Todd McArtor
<writer>	Danny Bryan
<digital artist>	Deb Sull
<photographer>	Mark Wiens
<programmer>	Stacey Schmitz
<creative director>	John Q. Harrington
<hardware>	Apple Macintosh
<software>	Adobe Photoshop
	JAVA Script
	Macromedia Freehand

</frameset>
<noframes>

</pageref>
<94><lhp>

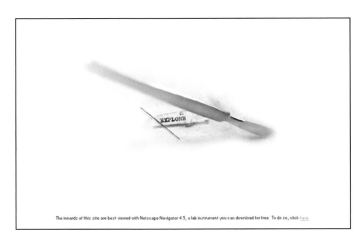

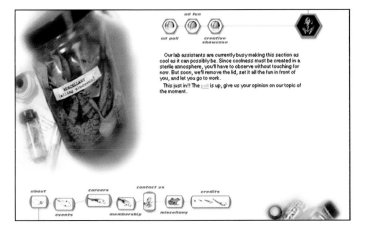

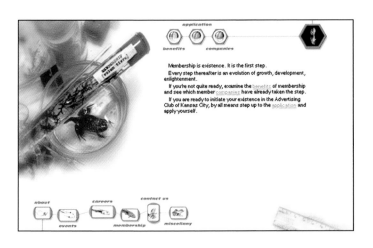

<warts and all> Juicy frog innards. That probably sums it up best. We could make up a bunch of stupid puns about frogs and dissection, but that would be dumb. Like, for instance, if we said, "Using frog dissection as a theme, this web site invites visitors to poke, prod and explore the inner workings of the Advertising Club of Kansas City, warts and all. The guts of the site were created on Macintosh G3 computers, designed with Photoshop and Freehand, programmed in Java Script, and kept fresh through the generous use of formaldehyde."

<pointy tool operator> Pretty dumb, huh? Puns are so 1980. It's all about concept today. See, the concept here is that we're giving people a deeper look inside the KC Ad Club. The frog represents the Ad Club. The pointy tools represent pointy tools. And you represent the pointy tool operator.

<we'll draw you> For a more in-depth explanation, send an e-mail. We'll draw you a picture. Until then, just remember "juicy frog innards." That's all you really need to know.

>

\<category\>	Non-Profit Organizations-Other Digital Advertising\</head\>
\<award\>	Gold\</title\>
\<agency\>	Nicholson NY/New York
\<client\>	The Mashantucket Pequot Nation
\<art directors\>	Guido Jimenez, Maya Kopytman
\<writers\>	Marshall Curry, Fred Lee, Ian Van Tuyl
\<digital artists\>	Matt Beringer, Kristine Yoonmi Chi, Kevin Chiu, Leslie Dan, Guido Jimenez, Maya Kopytman, Connie Lee, Michael Morse, Mario Sermonetta, Marianna Trofimava
\<photographers\>	Jim Brill, Emma Ross
\<producers\>	Jim Brill, Jonathan Spangler, Ian Van Tuyl
\<multimedia\>	Jonathan Alberts, Jim Brill, Raymond Dougherty, Alberto Forero, Liju Huang Jiro Ietaka, Yun Rhee, Mayumi Sato, Carolyn Schutz, Tom Walker
\<programmers\>	Jiro Ietaka, Wells Packard, Jim Powers
\<creative director\>	Tom Nicholson
\<hardware\>	Avid, PC, SGI
\<software\>	Adobe AfterEffects, Adobe Illustrator, Adobe Premier, Alias Macromedia Director, Macromedia SoundEdit, Sound Forge

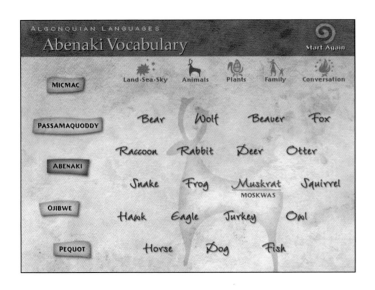

\<variety of content\>

Over the course of four years, Nicholson NY designed and produced a series of content-rich interactive programs for the Mashantucket Pequot Museum and Research Center's permanent exhibits. The six programs, accessible at 23 stations, cover topics ranging from the geological history and natural resources of Southern New England to the social and political history of the Mashantucket Pequot Nation. Touch-screens allow users to easily navigate a variety of content, including 3-D computer animations, documentary footage, traditional media and even hand-painted cell animations— all viewed in broadcast-quality digital video.

\<the most casual user\>

Nicholson's interactives are accurate even down to the native tree bark depicted in the 3-D models —realism that might be lost on some users, but is not lost on scholars who use the museum for research. Although each program has hours of content, even the most casual user can gain valuable information by spending only minutes with any one program.

\<make imaginative use\>

The interactives are the most extensive programs of their kind. They make imaginative use of technology and extend the museum's ability to communicate with visitors and provide them with engaging and informative experiences.

\<br\>

What's Heroin really like?

Forward ▷

\<html\>
\<head\>

\<category\>	Non-Profit Organizations-Other Digital Advertising\</head\>
\<award\>	Silver\</title\>
\<agency\>	Leo Burnett/Singapore
\<client\>	National Council Against Drug Abuse
\<art director\>	Ding Yew Moong
\<writer\>	Graham Kelly
\<digital artist\>	Valerie Ng
\<producer\>	Richard McCabe
\<multimedia\>	Human Interaction Technologies (HIT)
\<programmer\>	Valerie Ng
\<creative director\>	Graham Kelly
\<hardware\>	PC
\<software\>	Adobe Illustrator
	Adobe Photoshop
	Macromedia Director

\</frameset\>
\<noframes\>
\<br\>\<br\>

<all euphoric> Doing ads about drugs is probably a little bit like doing drugs themselves. You start out all euphoric. And then you come down. Because every good idea you come up with seems to have been done already.

<the point about loss> Luckily, the Net opened up a fresh way of doing things. It let us take a simple proposition ("Heroin will take control of your life") and make it more compelling. We developed three interactive programs, each of which made the point about loss of control in a different way. (For instance in one program, the "forward" button works, but not the "back" button).

<the "ad radar"> We then e-mailed them to young Singaporeans. Recipients were asked to pass them on to friends. So the work spread very quickly over the Net. This also enabled us to slip under the "ad radar", because it didn't seem like government propaganda. It was an e-mail from a friend.

>

</pageref>
<99><rhp>

<award>
<Silver> </pic>

excerpt from
Mexican Loneliness
by Jack Kerouac

if I walk my foot breaks down
if I smile my masks a farce
if I cry I'm just a child
if I remember I'm a liar
if I write the writing's done
if I die the dying's over
if I live the dying's just begun
if I wait the waiting's longer
if I go the going's gone

<html>
<head>

<category>	Student Competition-Other Digital Advertising</head>
<award>	Silver</title>
<client>	Jack Kerouac Promotion
<art director>	Douglas Parker
<writer>	Douglas Parker
<digital artist>	Douglas Parker
<producer>	Douglas Parker
<multimedia>	Douglas Parker
<programmer>	Douglas Parker
<hardware>	Apple Macintosh
<software>	Adobe Photoshop HyperStudio

</frameset>
<noframes>

</pageref>
<100><lhp>

I only wanted one thing from my interactive design: for Jack Kerouac to influence others the way he influenced me.

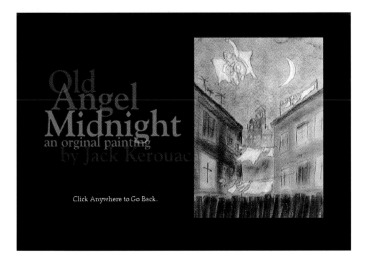

<award>
<merit winners>

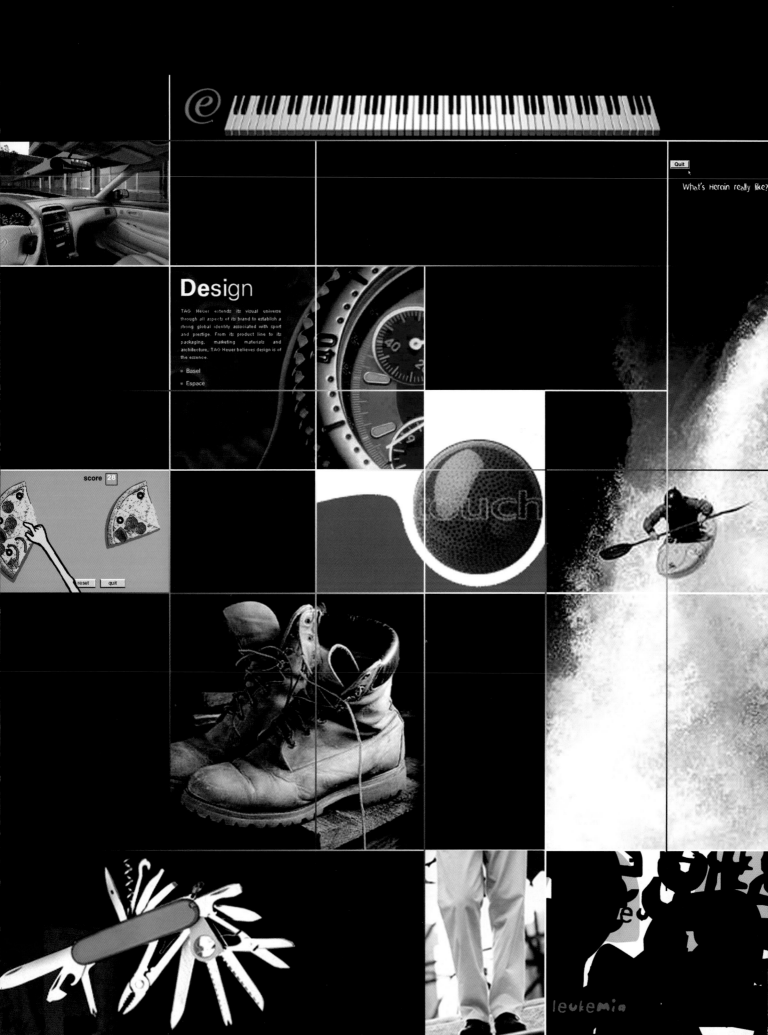

Quit

What's Heroin really like?

Design

TAG Heuer extends its visual universe through all aspects of its brand to establish a strong global identity associated with sport and prestige. From its product line to its packaging, marketing materials and architecture, TAG Heuer believes design is of the essence.

◦ Basel
◦ Espace

score 28

reset   quit

leukemia

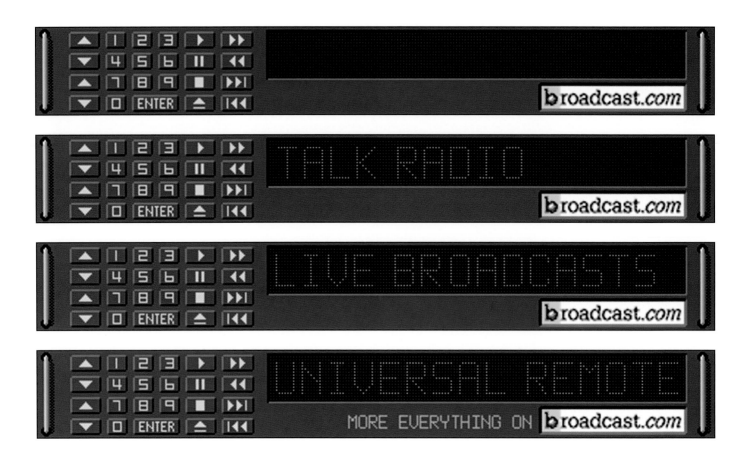

<html>
<head>

<category>	Banner-Link Only Single</head>
<award>	Merit</title>
<agency>	Click Here/Dallas
<client>	Broadcast.com
<url>	www.clickhere.com/oneshow/remote/
<art director>	Marcus Slaven
<writer>	Henry Popp
<hardware>	Apple Macintosh
<software>	Adobe ImageReady Adobe Photoshop

</frameset>
<noframes>

</pageref>
<102><thp>

<html>
<head>

<category>	Banner-Link Only Single</head>
<award>	Merit</title>
<agency>	Cohn & Wells/San Francisco
<client>	Sony
<url>	www.cohn-wells.com/retrospective/sony/ 239_mavica/index.html
<art director>	Simon Nickson
<writer>	Drummond Berman
<digital artist>	Jonathan Rose
<producer>	Jake Mora
<hardware>	Apple Macintosh PC
<software>	Adobe Photoshop Gif Builder

</frameset>
<noframes>

</pageref>
103 <rhp>

<html>
<head>

>

<category>	Banner-Link Only Single</head>
<award>	Merit</title>
<agency>	Euro RSCG DSW Partners/Salt Lake City
<client>	Intel
<url>	www.dsw.com/oneshow/xeon
<art director>	Heather Brown
<writer>	Muffy Ferro
<digital artist>	Matt Davis
<producer>	Aaron Ozminski
<programmer>	Freestyle
<creative director>	Heather Brown
<hardware>	PC
<software>	Adobe Photoshop

</frameset>
<noframes>

</pageref>
<104><lhp>

<head>
<category>Banner-Link Only Single</head>

<html>
<head>

<category>	Banner-Link Only Single</head>
<award>	Merit</title>
<agency>	Euro RSCG DSW Partners/Salt Lake City
<client>	IOMEGA
<url>	www.dsw.com/oneshow/recordit
<art director>	Stephen Thompson
<writer>	Joe Totten
<digital artist>	Matt Davis
<photographer>	Matt Davis
<producer>	Aaron Ozminski
<creative director>	Stephen Thompson
<hardware>	PC
<software>	Adobe Photoshop Uleaded Gif Animator

</frameset>
<noframes>

</pageref>
<105><rhp>

<html>
<head>

<category>	Banner-Link Only Single</head>
<award>	Merit</title>
<agency>	Hill Holliday Interactive/Boston
<client>	Lotus
<art directors>	Dmitri Cavander Dave Laucirica
<writers>	Vashti Brotherhood Jim Milke
<digital artist>	Michael Lotenero
<multimedia>	Mike Jeffers
<hardware>	PC
<software>	Adobe Illustrator Adobe Photoshop Equilibrium Debabelizer Macromedia Director NT

</frameset>
<noframes>

</pageref>
<106><lhp>

<head>
<category>Banner-Link Only Single</head>

EARTH

Our Customer Support Center is open
24 hours a day

MARS

Our Customer Support Center is open
24 hours 37 minutes a day

VENUS

Our Customer Support Center is open
5,832 hours 30 minutes a day

WANG
GLOBAL

Choose Wang Global for ODIN. _ click here> odin.wang.com

<html>
<head>

<category>	Banner-Link Only Single</head>
<award>	Merit</title>
<agency>	Hill Holliday Interactive/Boston
<client>	Wang Global
<art director>	Dave Laucirica
<writer>	Jim Milke
<hardware>	Apple Macintosh
<software>	Adobe Illustrator
	Adobe Photoshop
	Equilibrium Debabelizer
	GifBuilder
	Lotus Avian Streaming Media
	Lotus Domino
	Lotus Notes

</frameset>
<noframes>

</pageref>
<107><rhp>

<head>
<category>Banner-Link Only Single</head>

<html>
<head>

>

<category>	Banner-Link Only Single</head>
<award>	Merit</title>
<agency>	Hill Holliday/Altschiller/New York
<client>	The Mining Company
<url>	www.HHANYC.com/miningco/miningco.html
<art director>	Trish Daley
<writer>	Sam Mazur
<creative directors>	Steve St. Clair David Altschiller
<hardware>	Apple Macintosh
<software>	Adobe Photoshop Gif Builder

</frameset>
<noframes>

</pageref>
<108><lhp>

`<html>`
`<head>`

`>`

`<category>`	Banner-Link Only Single`</head>`
`<award>`	Merit`</title>`
`<agency>`	Lowe & Partners/SMS/New York, San Francisco
`<client>`	Sun Microsystems
`<url>`	38.245.119.101/sun/index.html
`<art director>`	Grace Lerner
`<writer>`	Jay Sharfstein
`<digital artist>`	Simon Crab
`<producers>`	Jon Bains Todd Moritz
`<multimedia>`	Lateral Net/London
`<programmer>`	Lee Coomber
`<creative directors>`	Lee Garfinkel Gary Goldsmith Peter Cohen Dean Hacohen
`<hardware>`	Apple Macintosh PC
`<software>`	Adobe Photoshop Java Development Tools Macromedia Director

`</frameset>`
`<noframes>`
`<br><br>`

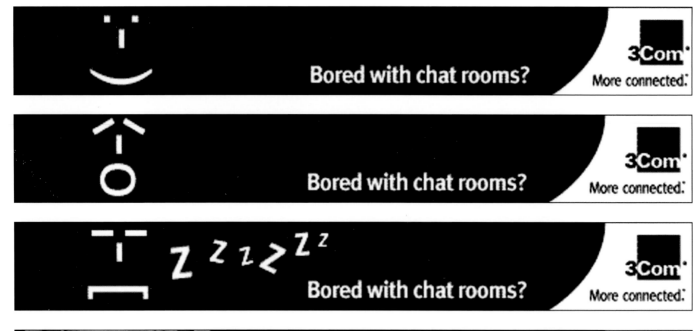

<html>
<head>

<category>	Banner-Link Only Single</head>
<award>	Merit</title>
<agency>	Modem Media.Poppe Tyson/Chicago
<client>	3Com
<art director>	Doug Fitzsimmons
<writer>	Steve Tullis
<digital artist>	Doug Fitzsimmons
<producer>	Michael Borsari
<creative director>	Charles Marrelli
<hardware>	Apple Macintosh
<software>	Adobe Illustrator Adobe Photoshop Equilibrium Debabilizer Gif Builder JAVA

</frameset>
<noframes>

</pageref>
<110><lhp>

Office DEPOT.com

CLICK HERE

REMEMBER TO PICK UP FAX PAPER

FOLDERS ENVELOPES PICK HIGHLIGHTERS PER CLIPS

TAKING CARE OF THESE JUST GOT EASIER

<html>
<head>

<category>	Banner-Link Only Single</head>
<award>	Merit</title>
<agency>	RockPile Interactive/San Francisco
<client>	Office Depot.Com
<art director>	Kevin M. Newby
<writer>	Doug McDermott
<hardware>	Apple Macintosh
<software>	Adobe Illustrator
	Adobe Photoshop
	Gif Animator

</frameset>
<noframes>

</pageref>
<111><rhp>

<html>
<head>

>

<category>	Banner-Link Only Campaign</head>
<award>	Merit</title>
<agency>	Bozell Worldwide/Southfield
<client>	Little Caesars
<url>	www.webspot.com/awards/banners/caesarbanners2.html
<art directors>	Geoffrey Gates Peter Arndt
<writers>	John Gregory Dan Sicko
<digital artist>	Geoffrey Gates
<producer>	Kathleen Starr
<multimedia>	Geoffrey Gates
<programmer>	Geoffrey Gates
<creative directors>	Gary Topolewski Husam Ajluni John Gregory Peter Arndt
<hardware>	Apple Macintosh
<software>	Macromedia Fireworks

</frameset>
<noframes>

</pageref>
<112><lhp>

<html>
<head>

<category>	Banner-Link Only Campaign</head>
<award>	Merit</title>
<agency>	CKS Partners/Portland
<client>	Mitsubishi Motor Sales of America
<url>	pdx.cks.com/99/ads/
<art director>	Michael Crossley
<writer>	Bill Weinstein
<digital artists>	Jeff Keyser Christian Worley Andrew Portello
<producer>	Jeff Keyser
<programmer>	Jeff Keyser
<creative directors>	Michael Crossley Bill Weinstein
<hardware>	Adobe Macintosh PC
<software>	Adobe Photoshop BBedit Equilibrium Debabelizer

</frameset>
<noframes>

</pageref>
<113><rhp>

<head>
<category>Banner-Link Only Campaign</head>

This pair of pliers has your name all over it.

Fortunately, it has this name all over it too.

CRAFTSMAN

Order this or any of over 3500 quality Craftsman tools right here.

CRAFTSMAN

<html>
<head>

<category>	Banner-Link Only Campaign</head>
<award>	Merit</title>
<agency>	Four Points Digital/Chicago
<client>	Sears, Roebuck and Company
<url>	www.four-points.com/showcase/oneshow.html
<art directors>	Pierre St-Jacques Todd Lemmon
<hardware>	PC
<software>	Adobe Photoshop Equilibrium Debabelizer Gif Builder

</frameset>
<noframes>

</pageref>
<114><lhp>

11:30 pm, The Red Eye.

Easy, inexpensive Web workspaces for your team.

Point, Click, Collaborate.
\<click here\>

\<html\>
\<head\>

\<category\>	Banner-Link Only Campaign\</head\>
\<award\>	Merit\</title\>
\<agency\>	Hill Holliday Interactive/Boston
\<client\>	Lotus
\<art director\>	Dmitri Cavander
\<writer\>	Vashti Brotherhood
\<digital artist\>	Justin Moore
\<hardware\>	Apple Macintosh
\<software\>	Adobe Photoshop
	Adobe Illustrator
	Equilibrium Debabelizer
	GifBuilder

\</frameset\>
\<noframes\>
\<br\>\<br\>

<head>
<category>Banner-Link Only Campaign</head>

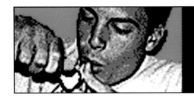

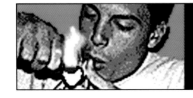

<html>
<head>

<category>	Banner-Link Only Campaign</head>
<award>	Merit</title>
<agency>	Left Field/San Francisco
<client>	Infoseek
<art director>	Paula Mills
<writer>	Greg Mills
<digital artist>	Paula Mills
<creative director>	Fred Schwartz
<hardware>	Apple Macintosh
<software>	Adobe ImageReady
	Adobe Photoshop

</frameset>
<noframes>

</pageref>
<116><lhp>

<html>
<head>

<category>	Banner-Link Only Campaign</head>
<award>	Merit</title>
<agency>	Lot21 Interactive Advertising/San Francisco
<client>	Daewoo Motor America Inc.
<url>	www.lot21.com/public/osi/daewoo/
<programmer>	Sasha Pave
<creative director>	Paco Vinoly
<hardware>	Apple Macintosh
<software>	Adobe Photoshop Macromedia Fireworks Macromedia Flash

</frameset>
<noframes>

</pageref>
<117><rhp>

Standard features:
improved social skills.

Standard features:
envious friends.

Standard features:
more dates.

Register to win a
NEW BEETLE® at Bank One.

<html>
<head>

>

<category>	Banner-Link Only Campaign</head>
<award>	Merit</title>
<agency>	Martin Interactive/Richmond
<client>	Bank One
<url>	www.martininteractive.com/work.html
<art directors>	Dave Parrish Robbie Wagner
<writer>	Ronda Craig
<creative director>	Dave Parrish
<hardware>	Apple Macintosh
<software>	Adobe Photoshop Gif Builder

</frameset>
<noframes>

</pageref>
<118><lhp>

\<html\>
\<head\>

\<category\>	Banner-Link Only Campaign\</head\>
\<award\>	Merit\</title\>
\<agency\>	Martin Interactive/Richmond
\<client\>	Saab USA
\<url\>	www.martininteractive.com/work.html
\<art directors\>	Robbie Wagner Dave Parrish
\<writer\>	Darrell Kanipe
\<digital artist\>	Robbie Wagner
\<creative director\>	Dave Parrish
\<hardware\>	Apple Macintosh
\<software\>	Adobe Photoshop Gif Builder

\</frameset\>
\<noframes\>
\<br\>\<br\>

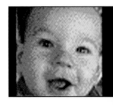

Working late again.
CLICK HERE FOR VIDEO CHAT. VIDEO MAIL. AND MORE.
3Com
More connected.

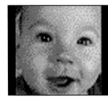
You can still put your baby to bed.
CLICK HERE FOR VIDEO CHAT. VIDEO MAIL. AND MORE.
3Com
More connected.

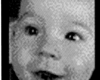
With **Bigpicture**™ Video
anything can happen
CLICK HERE FOR VIDEO CHAT. VIDEO MAIL. AND MORE.
3Com
More connected.

NO MORE BLIND DATES.
3Com
More connected.

With **Bigpicture**™ Video
anything can happen
CLICK HERE FOR VIDEO CHAT, VIDEO MAIL, AND MORE.
3Com
More connected.

<html>
<head>

<category>	Banner-Link Only Campaign</head>
<award>	Merit</title>
<agency>	Modem Media.Poppe Tyson/Chicago
<client>	3Com
<art directors>	Thomas McCue Doug Fitzsimmons
<writer>	Steve Tullis
<digital artist>	Doug Fitzsimmons
<producer>	Michael Borsari
<hardware>	Apple Macintosh

</frameset>
<noframes>

</pageref>
<120><lhp>

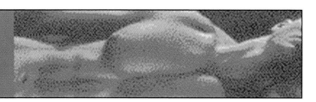

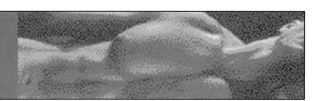

\<html\>
\<head\>

\<category\>	Banner-Link Only Campaign\</head\>
\<award\>	Merit\</title\>
\<agency\>	Thunder House/Cambridge
\<client\>	Durex
\<art director\>	Brenton Welsh
\<writers\>	Marty Kaufman Michael Solow
\<digital artist\>	Robert Napier
\<producer\>	Darcy Conlin
\<programmer\>	Tuna Chetterjee
\<hardware\>	Apple Macintosh
\</frameset\>	
\<noframes\>	
\<br\>\<br\>	

FAIRY TALE CONSULTANT

Read to a kid in the hospital.
Other high-level positions available.

CLICK HERE

KICK-BALL COMMISSIONER

Pitch in at an after-school sports program
Other high-level positions available.

CLICK HERE

\<html\>
\<head\>

\>

\<category\>	Banner-Link Only Campaign\</head\>
\<award\>	Merit\</title\>
\<agency\>	US Interactive/New York
\<client\>	Ad Council
\<url\>	www.usinteractive.com/adbanners
\<writer\>	Dave Keener
\<digital artist\>	David Haring
\<creative director\>	Bronson Smith
\<hardware\>	Apple Macintosh
\<software\>	Adobe Illustrator
Adobe Photoshop

\</frameset\>
\<noframes\>
\<br\>\<br\>

<head>
<category>Banner-Interactive Single</head>

<html>
<head>

<category>	Banner-Interactive Single</head>
<award>	Merit</title>
<agency>	Bent Media/New Orleans
<client>	McIlhenny Company, makers of Tabasco brand Pepper Sauce
<url>	www.intervu.net/richmedia/popup13.html
<art director>	Brad Brewster
<writer>	Julie Koppman
<digital artist>	Brad Brewster
<producer>	DDB Needham Worldwide/Dallas
<programmer>	IntervVU
<creative directors>	Brad Brewster Julie Koppman
<hardware>	Apple Macintosh PC
<software>	Adobe Illustrator Adobe Photoshop GifMation JAVA

</frameset>
<noframes>

</pageref>
<123><rhp>

<head>
<category>Banner-Interactive Single</head>

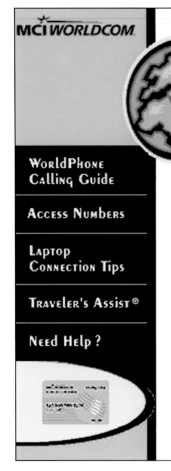

<html>
<head>

<category>	Banner-Interactive Single</head>
<award>	Merit</title>
<agency>	Messner Vetere Berger McNamee Schmetterer/Euro RSCG/New York
<client>	MCI Worldcom
<art director>	Chris Grayson
<writer>	Matthew Dikdan
<producer>	Chris Actis
<creative director>	Jason Lellos
<hardware>	Apple Macintosh
<software>	Adobe Illustrator
	Adobe Photoshop
	Macromedia Director
	Macromedia Flash

</frameset>
<noframes>

</pageref>
<124><lhp>

\<html\>
\<head\>

\<category\>	Banner-Interactive Single\</head\>
\<award\>	Merit\</title\>
\<agency\>	Ogilvy Interactive/New York
\<client\>	IBM
\<url\>	www.oandmi.com/media/eculture/work/showcase.html (username: media, password: banners)
\<art director\>	Warren Kemp
\<writer\>	David Levy
\<digital artist\>	Rachael Heapps
\<producers\>	Jude Raymond Fish Kate Kehoe
\<programmer\>	David Carson/Compound
\<creative director\>	Jan Leth
\<hardware\>	Apple Macintosh
\<software\>	Adobe Illustrator Adobe Photoshop Enliven Macromedia Director Macromedia Flash

\</frameset\>
\<noframes\>
\<br\>\<br\>

<head>
<category>Banner-Interactive Single</head>

Can the hands of a virtuoso reach across the web?
Sure. But it's not a solo effort.

www.yamaha.com is an IBM e-business.
Click here to hear.

eric johnson

director
yamaha artist services
www.yamaha.cor

IBM. e-business @.
Case studies | The e-business mark | Contact IBM

<html>
<head>

<category>	Banner-Interactive Single</head>
<award>	Merit</title>
<agency>	Ogilvy Interactive/New York
<client>	IBM
<url>	www.oandmi.com/media/eculture/work/showcase.html (username: media, password: banners)
<art director>	Warren Kemp
<writer>	David Levy
<digital artist>	Rachael Heapps
<producers>	Jude Raymond Fish Kate Kehoe
<programmer>	David Carson/Compound
<creative director>	Jan Leth
<hardware>	Apple Macintosh
<software>	Adobe Illustrator Adobe Photoshop Enliven Macromedia Director Macromedia Flash

</frameset>
<noframes>

</pageref>
126><lhp>

<head>
<category>Banner-Interactive Single</head>

<html>
<head>

<category>	Banner-Interactive Single</head>
<award>	Merit</title>
<agency>	RockPile Interactive/San Francisco
<client>	Berkeley Systems
<art director>	Kevin M. Newby
<writer>	Justin Merickel
<hardware>	Apple Macintosh
<software>	Adobe Illustrator
	Adobe Photoshop
	Gif Animator

</frameset>
<noframes>

</pageref>
<127><rhp>

<html>
<head>

<category>	Banner-Interactive Single</head>
<award>	Merit</title>
<agency>	RockPile Interactive/San Francisco
<client>	Berkeley Systems
<art director>	Kevin M. Newby
<writer>	Doug McDermott
<hardware>	Apple Macintosh
<software>	Abobe Illustrator
	Adobe Photoshop
	Gif Animator

</frameset>
<noframes>

</pageref>
<128><lhp>

<html>
<head>

<category>	Banner-Interactive Campaign</head>
<award>	Merit</title>
<agency>	IN2/New York
<client>	Red Rocket
<url>	www.in2.com/oneclub/1998/redrocket/
<art director>	Carol Chow
<writer>	Marc Landau
<digital artists>	Paul Johnson Danny Hobart
<producer>	Jeff Kolber
<creative director>	Carol Chow
<hardware>	Apple Macintosh
<software>	Adobe Illustrator Adobe ImageReady Adobe Photoshop BBEdit Macromedia Director

</frameset>
<noframes>

</pageref>
<129><rhp>

\<html>
\<head>

\<category>	Banner-Interactive Campaign\</head>
\<award>	Merit\</title>
\<agency>	Interactive8/New York
\<client>	M&M/Mars
\<url>	www.interactive8.com/one
\<art director>	David Lewis
\<writer>	Jonathan Lewis
\<digital artist>	David Lewis
\<producer>	Stephanie Chin
\<hardware>	Apple Macintosh
\<software>	Adobe Photoshop Gif Builder

\</frameset>
\<noframes>
\
\

<head>
<category>Beyond the Banner</head>

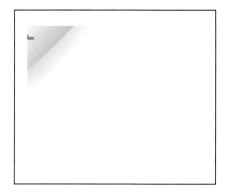
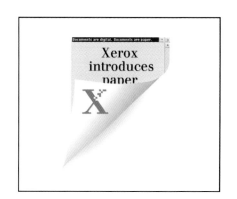

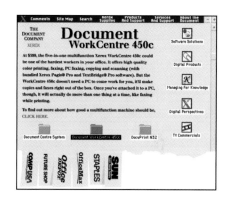

<html>
<head>

<category>	Beyond the Banner</head>
<award>	Merit</title>
<agency>	Brand Dialogue(Y&R)/New York
<client>	Xerox
<url>	www.stage.brand-dialogue.com/xerox/
<art director>	Delia Moran
<writer>	Sean Skilling
<digital artist>	Michele Marx
<producer>	Craig Marrano
<programmer>	Craig Marrano
<creative director>	Sean Skilling
<hardware>	Apple Macintosh PC
<software>	Adobe Photoshop Allaire Homesite BBEdit Go Live CyberStudio Macromedia AfterShock Macromedia Flash

</frameset>
<noframes>

</pageref>
<131><rhp>

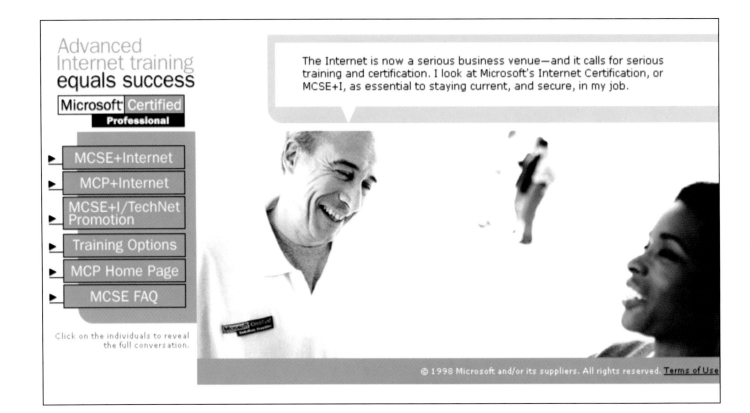

\<html\>
\<head\>

\<category\>	Beyond the Banner\</head\>
\<award\>	Merit\</title\>
\<agency\>	Cohn & Wells/San Francisco
\<client\>	Microsoft
\<url\>	205.162.10.4/cm/retrospective/iis/ ms353/buffer/default2.asp
\<art director\>	Andy Davis
\<writer\>	Cynthia Robinson
\<digital artist\>	David Pinault
\<producer\>	Brad Benton
\<programmer\>	David Pinault
\<hardware\>	Apple Macintosh PC
\<software\>	BBEdit Java Script

\</frameset\>
\<noframes\>
\<br\>\<br\>

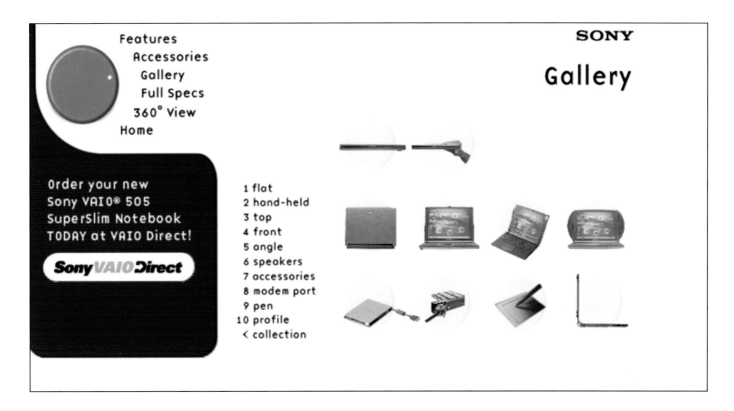

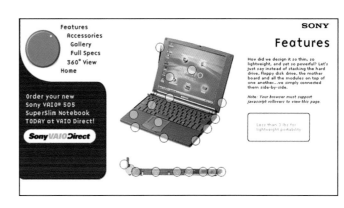

<html>
<head>

<category>	Beyond the Banner</head>
<award>	Merit</title>
<agency>	Cohn & Wells/San Francisco
<client>	Sony
<url>	www.sony.com/505
<art director>	Brad Benton
<writer>	Jana Bender
<producer>	Jake Mora
<programmers>	David Pinault Gilles Baltrusitis
<hardware>	Apple Macintosh PC
<software>	Adobe Photoshop, Gif Builder HTML, Quicktime VR

</frameset>
<noframes>

</pageref>
<133><rhp>

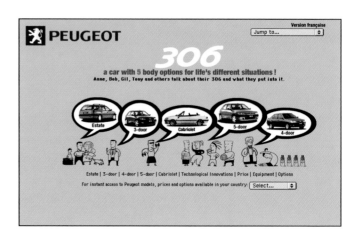

<html>
<head>

<category>	Beyond the Banner</head>
<award>	Merit</title>
<agency>	Connectworld/Paris
<client>	Peugeot Automobiles
<url>	www.peugeot.com
<art director>	Laurent Thomas-Gerard
<writer>	Randall Koral
<digital artist>	Thomas Aubrun
<producer>	Angelique Provost
<programmers>	Frederic Dufils Paul Demare Charles Rouillon
<creative directors>	Laurent Thomas-Gerard Randall Koral
<hardware>	Apple Macintosh PC
<software>	Adobe Photoshop Allaire Homesite Hotdog

</frameset>
<noframes>

</pageref>
<134><lhp>

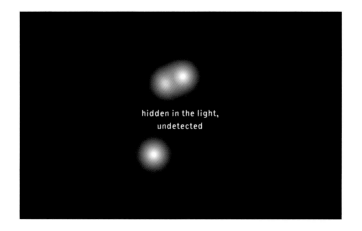

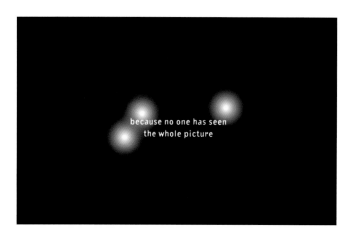

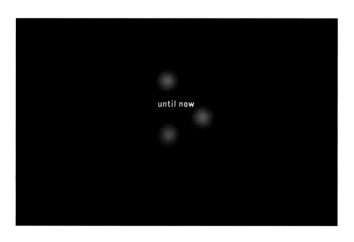

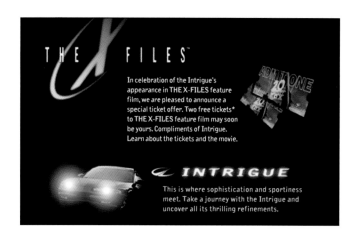

<html>
<head>

<category>	Beyond the Banner</head>
<award>	Merit</title>
<agency>	Giant Step/Chicago
<client>	Oldsmobile Intrigue
<digital artist>	Geoff Petkus
<art director>	Sean Moran
<writer>	Sean Moran
<producer>	Rob Murray
<creative director>	Geoff Petkus
<hardware>	Apple Macintosh PC
<software>	Adobe Illustrator Adobe Photoshop Macromedia Flash Microsoft Visual Studio

</frameset>
<noframes>

</pageref>
<135><rhp>

<html>
<head>

<category>	Beyond the Banner</head>
<award>	Merit</title>
<agency>	I-traffic/New York
<client>	Beyond.com
<url>	www.i-traffic.com/awards/jason
<art director>	Steve Divins/The Chopping Block
<writers>	Rudy Grahn
	Justin Kaswan
<digital artist>	Jason Parkin
<photographer>	Rob Reed
<producer>	Steve Divins
<programmer>	Steve Divins
<hardware>	Apple Macintosh
<software>	Adobe ImageReady
	Adobe Photoshop
	GoLive Cyberstudio

</frameset>
<noframes>

</pageref>

<lhp>

`<html>`
`<head>`

`<category>`	Beyond the Banner`</head>`
`<award>`	Merit`</title>`
`<agency>`	Lowe & Partners/SMS/New York, San Francisco
`<client>`	Sun Microsystems
`<url>`	38.245.119.101/sun/index.html
`<art directors>`	Peter Cohen Michael Thomas
`<writers>`	Andrew Baker Kurtis Glade
`<digital artist>`	John Wier
`<producers>`	Lisa Herbert Todd Moritz
`<multimedia>`	SF Interactive
`<programmer>`	Matisse Enzer
`<creative directors>`	Lee Garfinkel Gary Goldsmith Peter Cohen Dean Hacohen
`<hardware>`	Apple Macintosh, PC
`<software>`	Adobe Photoshop Java Development Tools Macromedia Director

DRAG THE TUBA ONTO
THE OSTRICH.

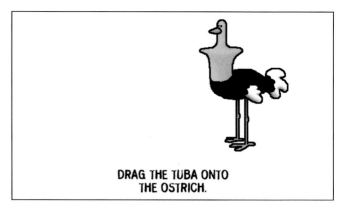

DRAG THE TUBA ONTO
THE OSTRICH.

DRAG THE TAP SHOES ONTO
THE DONKEY.

DRAG THE TAP SHOES ONTO
THE DONKEY.

DRAG THE OPERA HELMET ONTO
NICK THE BUTCHER.

CONGRATULATIONS. YOU JUST EXPERIENCED HOW
SIMPLE IT IS TO BUILD INTERNET ACCESS INTO YOUR CONSUMER
DEVICES. INTRODUCING PERSONAL WEBACCESS.

CLICK HERE FOR MORE INFORMATION.

<html>
<head>

<category>	Beyond the Banner</head>
<award>	Merit</title>
<agency>	Lowe & Partners/SMS/New York, San Francisco
<client>	Sun Microsystems
<url>	38.245.119.101/sun/index.html
<art director>	Michael Thomas
<writer>	Chris Stoltz
<digital artist>	Zack Sudderth
<multimedia>	Art & Science
<creative directors>	Lee Garfinkel, Gary Goldsmith, Peter Cohen, Dean Hacohen
<hardware>	Apple Macintosh, PC
<software>	Adobe Photoshop, Java Development Tools, Macromedia Director

</frameset>
</pageref>   <noframes>
<138><lhp>

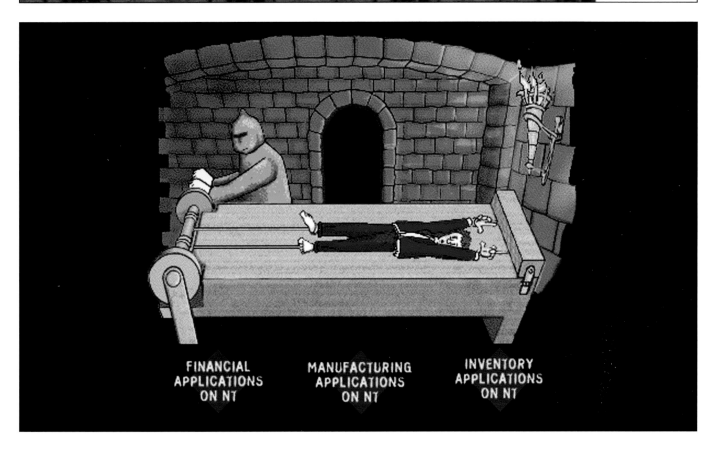

<html>
<head>

<category>	Beyond the Banner</head>
<award>	Merit</title>
<agency>	Lowe & Partners/SMS/New York, San Francisco
<client>	Sun Microsystems
<url>	38.245.119.101/sun/index.html
<art director>	Grace Lerner
<writer>	Jay Sharfstein
<digital artist>	Simon Crab
<producers>	Jon Bains Todd Moritz
<multimedia>	Lateral Net/London
<programmer>	Simon Crab
<creative directors>	Lee Garfinkel Gary Goldsmith Peter Cohen Dean Hacohen
<hardware>	Apple Macintosh, PC
<software>	Adobe Photoshop, Java Development Tools, Macromedia Director

</frameset>
<noframes>

</pageref>
<139><rhp>

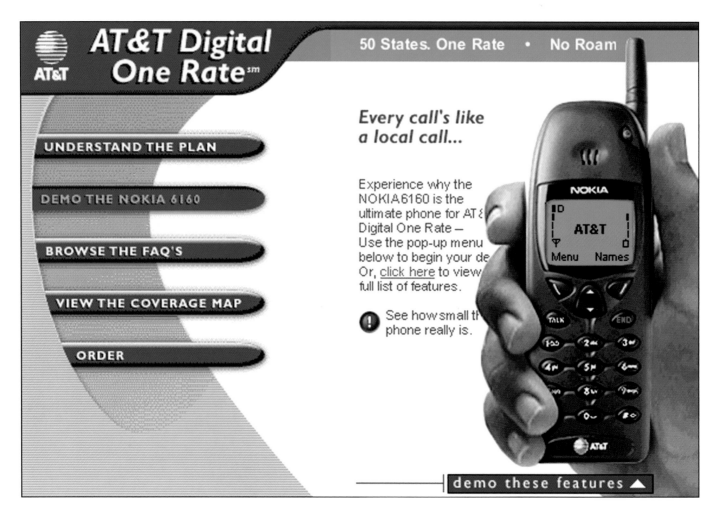

<html>
<head>

<category>	Beyond the Banner</head>
<award>	Merit</title>
<agency>	Modem Media.Poppe Tyson/Norwalk
<client>	AT&T Digital One Rate Wireless Service
<art directors>	Lilian Rousseau, Jonathan Damato, Lisa Parett
<writer>	Kitti Borgatti
<producer>	Bob Carilli
<programmer>	Anthony Krinsky
<creative directors>	Tom Beeby, Peter Rivera
<hardware>	Apple Macintosh, PC
<software>	Adobe Photoshop, DHTML, GifBuilder, HTML Java Script, Macromedia Shockwave

</frameset>
</pageref> <noframes>

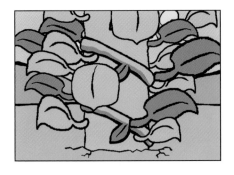

\<html>
\<head>

\<category>	Beyond the Banner\</head>
\<award>	Merit\</title>
\<agency>	Nicholson NY/New York
\<client>	IBM
\<url>	www.nny.com/awards/one_show_99
\<art director>	Britt Funderburk
\<writer>	Britt Funderburk
\<digital artist>	John Kaurderer
\<multimedia>	Jiro Ietaka
\<creative director>	Tom Nicholson
\<hardware>	Apple Macintosh
\<software>	Adobe Photoshop Equilibrium Debabilizer Macromedia Director Macromedia SoundEdit 16

\</frameset>
\<noframes>
\
\

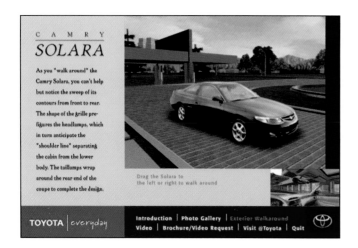

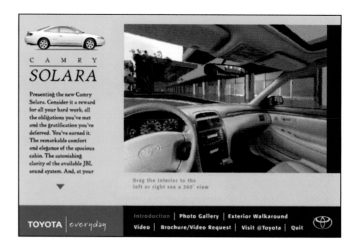

<html>
<head>

<category>	Beyond the Banner</head>
<award>	Merit</title>
<agency>	Saatchi & Saatchi/Los Angeles
<client>	Toyota Motor Sales, USA
<url>	www.saatchila.com/extras/oneshow
<art director>	Chris Ray
<writer>	Anthony Wells
<photographers>	Steve Cooper John Early
<producer>	Matt Mayer
<programmer>	Carolyn McDonald
<creative directors>	Dean Van Eimeren Alan Segal
<hardware>	Apple Macintosh
<software>	Adobe Image Ready Adobe Photoshop DHTML Java Script Macromedia Flash Macromedia SoundEdit 16

</frameset>
</pageref>   <noframes>
<142><lhp>

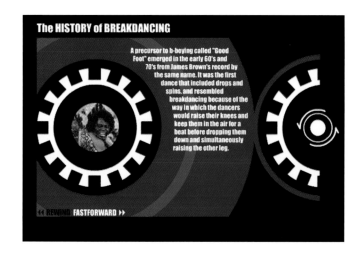

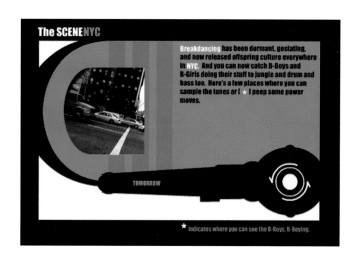

>

<html>
<head>

<category>	Promotional Advertising–Web Sites</head>
<award>	Merit</title>
<agency>	AGENCY.COM/New York
<client>	Urban Desires
<url>	www.desires.com/features/breaking
<art director>	Khoi Uong
<writers>	Khoi Uong, Laurie Linder
<digital artists>	Khoi Uong, Ryniee Auh
<photographers>	Khoi Uong, Kiley Bates
<producers>	Kiley Bates, James Plath, Kyle Shannon Chan Suh, Gabrielle Shannon
<multimedia>	Alison Strandwitz, James Plath Jean Esquirel, Kyle Shannon
<programmer>	Dheeraj Vasishta
<creative director>	PJ Loughran
<hardware>	Apple Macintosh PC
<software>	Macromedia Flash

</frameset>
<noframes>

</pageref>
<143><rhp>

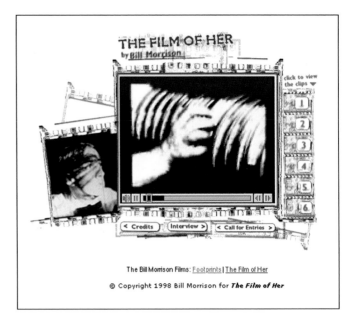

<html>
<head>

<category>	Promotional Advertising–Web Sites</head>
<award>	Merit</title>
<agency>	AGENCY.COM/New York
<client>	Urban Desires
<url>	www.desires.com/features/thefilmofher
<art director>	PJ Loughran
<digital artist>	Tom Moran
<producers>	Kiley Bates
	James Plath
	Kyle Shannon
	Chan Suh
	Gabrielle Shannon
<programmer>	Dheeraj Vasishta
<creative director>	PJ Loughran
<hardware>	Apple Macintosh
	PC
<software>	Adobe ImageReady
	Adobe Photoshop
	HTML
	Quicktime

</frameset>
<noframes>

</pageref>
<144><lhp>

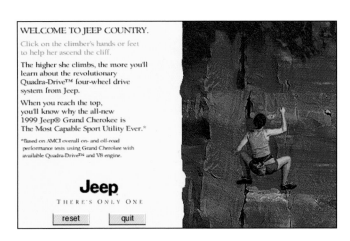

<html>
<head>

<category>	Promotional Advertising–Web Sites</head>
<award>	Merit</title>
<agency>	Bozell Worldwide/Southfield
<client>	Chrysler Corporation
<url>	www.webspot.com/jeep/climber
art director>	Scott Lange Peter Arndt
<writer>	John Gregory
<digital artist>	Dragonfly Studios
<photographer>	Brad Stanley
<producer>	Kathleen Starr
<multimedia>	Dragonfly Studios Main Street Multimedia The Industrial Zoo
<programmers>	Butler Graphics Main Street Multimedia
<creative directors>	Gary Topolewski, Bill Morden Husam Ajluni, John Gregory Peter Arndt
<hardware>	Apple Macintosh PC
<software>	Adobe Photoshop, Macromedia Director

</frameset>
<noframes>

</pageref>
<rhp>

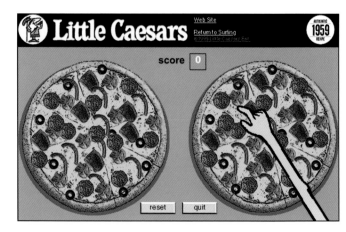

\<html\>
\<head\>

\<category\>	Promotional Advertising-Web Sites\</head\>
\<award\>	Merit\</title\>
\<agency\>	Bozell Worldwide/Southfield
\<client\>	Little Caesars
\<url\>	www.webspot.com/littlecaesars/nibbles
\<art directors\>	Geoffrey Gates Peter Arndt
\<writer\>	John Gregory
\<digital artist\>	Dragonfly Studios
\<producer\>	Kathleen Starr
\<multimedia\>	Dragonfly Studios Main Street Multimedia The Industrial Zoo
\<programmer\>	Dragonfly Studios Main Street Multimedia
\<creative directors\>	Gary Topolewski Husam Ajluni John Gregory Peter Arndt
\<hardware\>	Apple Macintosh, PC
\<software\>	Adobe Photoshop, Macromedia Director Macromedia Fireworks

\</frameset\>
\</pageref\> \<noframes\>
\<146\>\<lhp\> \<br\>\<br\>
\<br\>\<br\>

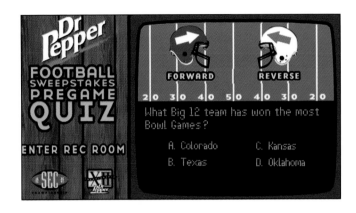

<html>
<head>

<category>	Promotional Advertising-Web Sites</head>
<award>	Merit</title>
<agency>	Brand Dialogue(Y&R)/New York
<client>	Dr. Pepper
<art director>	Delia Moran
<writer>	Todd Harrington
<digital artist>	Paula Wood
<producer>	Ted Kacandes
<programmer>	Ted Kacandes
<creative director>	Sean Skilling
<hardware>	Apple Macintosh PC
<software>	Adobe Illustrator Macromedia Flash PC-Homesite Editor

</frameset>
<noframes>

</pageref>
<147><rhp>

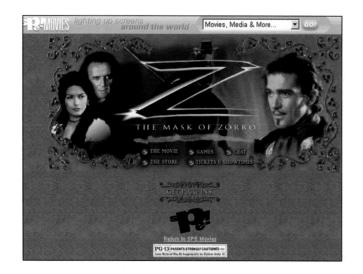

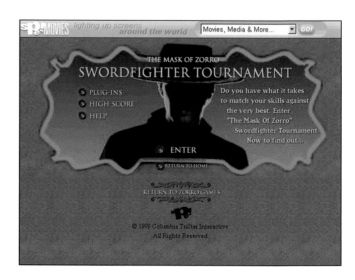

<html>

<head>

<category>	Promotional Advertising–Web Sites</head>
<award>	Merit</title>
<agency>	Columbia TriStar Interactive/Culver City
<client>	Columbia TriStar Interactive
<url>	www.sony.com/zorro
<producer>	Ira Rubenstein
<multimedia>	DNA Studio
<creative director>	John Moshay
<hardware>	Apple Macintosh PC
<software>	Adobe Illustrator Adobe Photoshop Live Picture Macromedia Director Macromedia Dreamweaver Macromedia Flash Visual SlickEdit

</frameset>

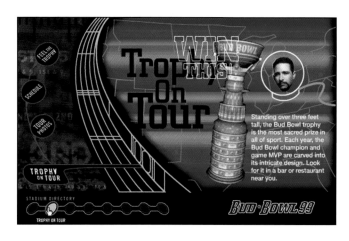

<html>
<head>

<category>	Promotional Advertising–Web Sites</head>
<award>	Merit</title>
<agency>	DDB Digital/Chicago
<client>	Anheuser-Busch
<url>	www.budbowl.com
<art directors>	Julian Wild
	Allen Morgenstern
	Brent Wilson
	Mark Masterson
<writers>	Robin Kurzer
	Steve Hunt
<producer>	Kelly Twohig
<multimedia>	Henderson Company
<programmers>	Joel Roller
	Rich Dettmer
<creative directors>	Brooke Narberg
	Mark Howell
	Steve Hunt
<hardware>	Apple Macintosh

</frameset>
<noframes>

<head>
<category>Promotional Advertising-Web Sites</head>

<html>
<head>

<category>	Promotional Advertising-Web Sites</head>
<award>	Merit</title>
<agency>	Duffy Design/Minneapolis
<client>	Nikon
<url>	www.nikonusa.com/proneas/
<art directors>	Dan Olson, Sida Phungjiam, Todd Bartz
<writers>	Debbie Gold, Kermit Cantwell
<digital artist>	Laurie Brown
<photographer>	Mark LaFavor
<producer>	Sarah Zanger
<multimedia>	Mark Sandau, Leslie Fandrich
<programmer>	Ariana French
<creative director>	Dan Olson
<hardware>	Apple Macintosh
<software>	Adobe Illustrator, Adobe Photoshop Coldfusion

</pageref>
<lhp>

</frameset>
<noframes>

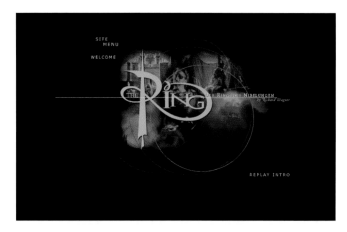

<html>
<head>

<category>	Promotional Advertising-Web Sites </head>
<award>	Merit </title>
<agency>	Euro RSCG DSW Partners/Salt Lake City
<client>	San Francisco Opera
<url>	www.dsw.com/oneshow/sfopera
<art directors>	Heather Brown Brad Eubanks Victoria Stanbach
<writers>	Jennifer Ward Chadwick Greenhalgh
<photographers>	Morton Larry Merkle Ron Schurl Matt Sohl
<producers>	Michael Aaron Ron Hendricks
<programmer>	Karen Tang
<creative directors>	Chadwick Greenhalgh Heather Brown
<hardware>	PC
<software>	Adobe Illustrator, Adobe Photoshop Allaire Homesite, Macromedia Flash

</frameset>
<noframes>

<html>
<head>

<category>	Promotional Advertising-Web Sites</head>
<award>	Merit</title>>
<agency>	Messner Vetere Berger McNamee Schnetterer/Euro RSCG/New York
<client>	Miramax Films
<url>	www.dimensionfilms.com/ows-doc/halloween:h20/index.html
<art director>	Eric Peterson
<writer>	Matthew Dikdan
<digital artist>	Eric Peterson
<producer>	Kim Lewis
<multimedia>	Logan Susnick
<programmer>	Logan Susnick
<creative director>	Jason Lellos
<hardware>	Apple Macintosh
<software>	Adobe Illustrator Adobe Photoshop Flash Technologies Macromedia Director

</frameset>
<noframes>

</pageref>
<152><lhp>

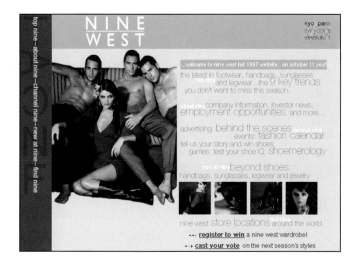

<html>
<head>

<category>	Promotional Advertising-Web Sites</head>
<award>	Merit</title>>
<agency>	Pittard Sullivan/Culver City
<client>	Nine West
<url>	www.ninewest.com
<art director>	Soo Chyun
<digital artist>	Soo Chyun
<photographer>	Herb Ritts
<producers>	Stephanie Otto, Julian Forniss
<programmers>	Jason Ramsey, John Foreman
<creative director>	Brian Black
<hardware>	Apple Macintosh PC Sun Solaris Spark Station
<software>	Adobe Illustrator, Adobe Photoshop BBEdit, Dynomorph Equilibrium Debabelizer HTML, Java Script

</frameset>
<noframes>

</pageref>
<153><rhp>

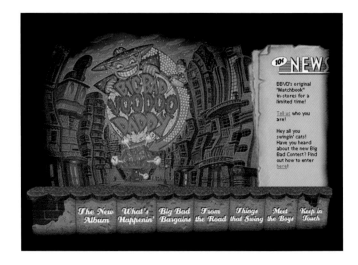

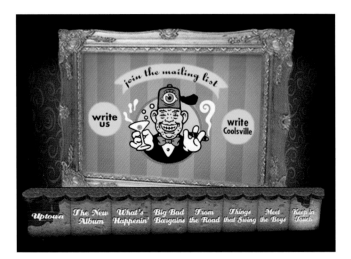

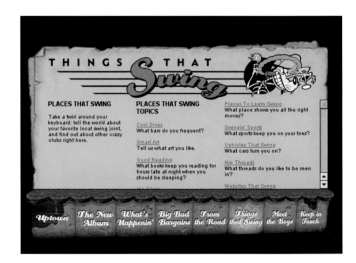

<html>
<head>

<category>	Promotional Advertising-WebSites</head>
<award>	Merit</title>
<agency>	Quantum Leap Communications/Chicago
<client>	Capitol Records
<url>	www.bbvd.com
<digital artist>	Andy Engel
<photographer>	Don Miller
<producers>	Brad Benedict Scotty Morris
<multimedia>	Mattie Langenberg Scott Kinsey
<programmers>	Mattle Langenberg, Scott Kinsey Robin Bechtel
<creative director>	Foredt Fein
<hardware>	Sun Server running Solaris OS
<software>	Adobe AfterEffects, Adobe Illustrator Adobe Photoshop, BBEdit, GifBuilder Macromedia Dreamweaver

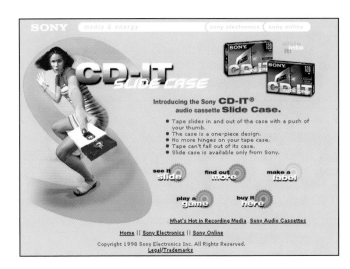

<html>
<head>

<category>	Promotional Advertising-Web Sites</head>
<award>	Merit</title>
<agency>	T3 Media/New York
<client>	Sony
<url>	www.sel.sony.com/SEL/rmeg/slide/index.html
<art director>	Leslie Sawin-Kepner
<digital artists>	Sherman Oh Sharon Mizota
<producer>	Abigail Carter
<multimedia>	Miles Dudgeon Dee Dixon
<programmer>	Shaque
<hardware>	Apple Macintosh
<software>	Adobe ImageReady Adobe Illustrator Adobe Photoshop Macromedia Director Macromedia Flash

</frameset>
<noframes>

 Faithful

 House broken

 Nose for the endzone

<html>
<head>

<category>	Promotional Advertising-Other Digital Advertising</head>
<award>	Merit</title>
<agency>	Ogilvy Interactive/New York
<client>	GTE
<url>	www.oandmi.com/ncaa/gte.dcr
<art directors>	Greg Kaplan Doug Miller
<writers>	Mark Goulding Patrick Clarke
<producer>	Sandy Donnelly
<creative director>	Jan Leth
<hardware>	Apple Macintosh
<software>	Adobe Illustrato Macromedia Director Macromedia Shockwave

</frameset>
<noframes>

</pageref>
<156><lhp>

\<html\>
\<head\>

\<category\>	Promotional Advertising-Other Digital Advertising\</head\>
\<award\>	Merit\</title\>
\<agency\>	Ogilvy Interactive/New York
\<client\>	IBM
\<url\>	www.oandmi.com/media/nagano_olympics/thrill.html (username: media, password: banners)
\<art director\>	Greg Kaplan
\<writer\>	Greg Kaplan
\<digital artist\>	Terrance Peng
\<producer\>	Kate Kehoe
\<creative director\>	Jan Leth
\<hardware\>	Apple Macintosh
\<software\>	Adobe Illustrator Macromedia Director Macromedia Shockwave

\</frameset\>
\<noframes\>
\<br\>\<br\>

<html>
<head>

<category>	Corporate Image Consumer-Web Sites </head>
<award>	Merit</title>
<agency>	ADJACENCY/San Francisco
<client>	TAG Heuer SA
<url>	www.tagheuer.com
<art directors>	Andrew Sather Bernie DeChant
<writer>	Michael Funkhauser
<digital artists>	Dave Le Andrew Sather
<producers>	Nick Folger Jen Wolf Leni Litonjua
<programmers>	Carlo Calica Matt Kirchstein
<creative director>	Andrew Sather
<hardware>	Apple Macintosh
<software>	Adobe Illustrator Adobe Photoshop BBEdit

</frameset>
</pageref>   <noframes>
<lhp>

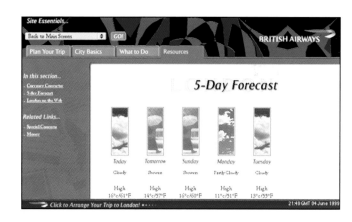

<html>
<head>

<category>	Corporate Image Consumer-Web Sites </head>
<award>	Merit</title>
<agency>	AGENCY.COM/New York
<client>	British Airways
<url>	www.british-airways.com
<art directors>	Jean Esquivel PJ Loughran
<writer>	Elisa Niemack
<digital artists>	Tom Moran John Nack Nate Harrison
<producers>	Megan McClelland, Dru Damico, Joanne Brunn Jennifer Pierce, Susan Shaughnessy, Jodi Lekacos
<programmers>	Nick Cook, Dheeraj Vasishta, Ralph Seaman
<creative directors>	Chris Needham, Laurent Stanevich James Plath, Sumin Chou
<hardware>	Apple Macintosh
<software>	Adobe Illustrator, Adobe ImageReady Adobe Photoshop, BBEdit, Macromedia Flash

</frameset>
<noframes>

</pageref>
<159><rhp>

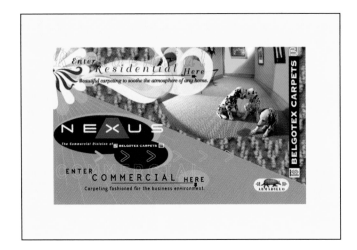
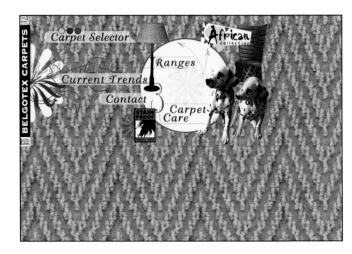

\<html\>
\<head\>

\<category\>	Corporate Image Consumer-Web Sites\</head\>
\<award\>	Merit\</title\>
\<agency\>	Armadillo Interactive/Durban
\<client\>	Belgotex carpets
\<url\>	www.nexuscarpets.co.za
\<art director\>	Stephen Embleton
\<writer\>	Justin Brown
\<photographer\>	Patrick McGee
\<producer\>	Duncan Forrest
\<multimedia\>	Stephen Embleton
\<programmer\>	Scott Dukes
\<creative director\>	Stephen Embleton
\<hardware\>	Apple Macintosh NT Server, PC
\<software\>	Adobe Photoshop Macromedia Flash Macromedia Freehand

\</frameset\>
\<noframes\>
\<br\>\<br\>

\</pageref\>

\<br\>\<br\>

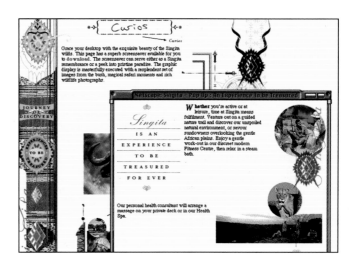

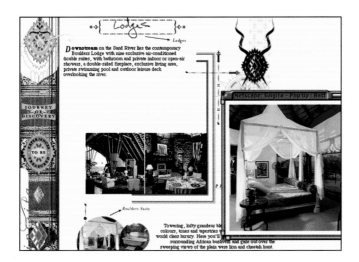

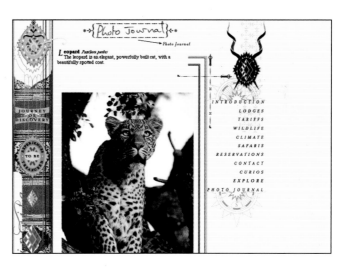

```
<html>
<head>
```

<category>	Corporate Image Consumer-Web Sites</head>
<award>	Merit</title>
<agency>	Armadillo Interactive/Durban
<client>	Singita Private Game Reserve
<url>	www.singita.co.za
<art directors>	Garth Walker Stephen Embleton
<writer>	Suzie Bell
<photographer>	Angie Buckland
<producer>	Duncan Forrest
<multimedia>	Stephen Embleton
<programmer>	Duncan Forrest
<creative director>	Stephen Embleton
<hardware>	Apple Macintosh NT Server PC
<software>	Adobe Photoshop, Macromedia Director Macromedia Freehand

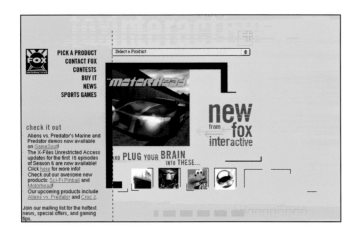

>

<html>
<head>

<category>	Corporate Image Consumer-Web Sites</head>
<award>	Merit</title>
<agency>	Circumstance/Big Hand/San Francisco
<client>	Fox Interactive
<url>	www.foxsportsgames.com
<art director>	Brian Kralyevich
<writers>	Molly Ditmore
	Priscilla Bournonnais
<digital artists>	Tim Barber
	David Bliss
	Josh Lowman
	George Rodgers
	Kaveh Soofi
	Fiel Valdez
<producer>	Natalie Ammirato
<multimedia>	Circumstance
<programmer>	Sean Rooney
<creative directors>	Tim Barber
	David Bliss
<hardware>	Apple Macintosh, PC
<software>	Adobe Illustrator, Adobe GoLive
	Adobe Photoshop

</frameset>
</pageref> <noframes>
162 <lhp>

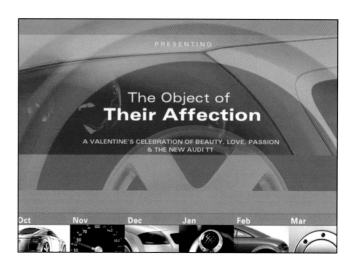

<html>
<head>

<category>	Corporate Image Consumer-Web Sites</head>
<award>	Merit</title>
<agency>	CKS Partners/New York
<client>	Audi of America
<url>	www.audiusa.com
<art directors>	Jeffrey Martin Kurt Thesing Hien Im
<writers>	Tom Keener Keith Byrne
<photographer>	Claudio Vasquez
<producer>	Michael Capecci
<programmer>	Network Publishing
<creative director>	Robert Wong
<hardware>	Apple Macintosh
<software>	Adobe Illustrator, Adobe Photoshop Macromedia Flash, Macromedia Shockwave

</frameset>
<noframes>

</pageref>
<163><rhp>

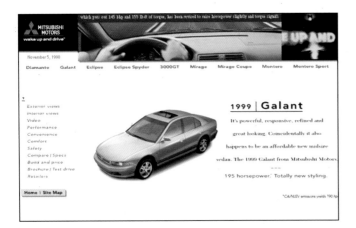

>

<html>
<head>

<category>	Corporate Image Consumer-Web Sites</head>
<award>	Merit</title>
<agency>	CKS Partners/Portland
<client>	Mitsubishi Motor Sales of America
<url>	www.mitsucars.com
<art directors>	Michael Crossley Richard Dunn
<writer>	Damien Geddry
<digital artists>	Richard Dunn, Jeff Keyser Christian Worley, Andrew Portello
<photographer>	EVOX Studios
<producers>	Jeff Keyser Tim Gault
<programmers>	David Welton Jeff Keyser Jaques Nadeau
<creative director>	Michael Crossley
<hardware>	Apple Macintosh, PC, UNIX
<software>	Adobe Photoshop, BBEdit Equilibrium Debabelizer, JAVA

</frameset>
<noframes>

</pageref>

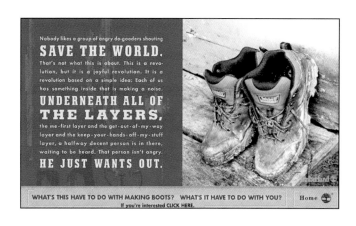

<html>
<head>

<category>	Corporate Image Consumer-Web Sites</head>
<award>	Merit</title>
<agency>	CKS Partners/Portland
<client>	Timberland
<url>	www.timberland.com
<art director>	Oscar Reza
<digital artist>	Oscar Reza
<producer>	TJ Cathey
<programmer>	Josh Hurwitz
<creative director>	Oscar Reza
<hardware>	Apple Macintosh PC SQL Server
<software>	Adobe Photoshop BBEdit Equilibrium Debabilizer MultiEdit

</frameset>
<noframes>

</pageref>
<165><rhp>

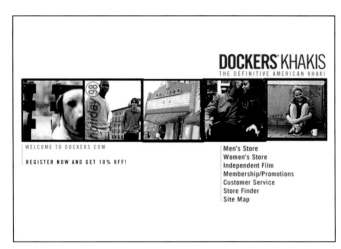

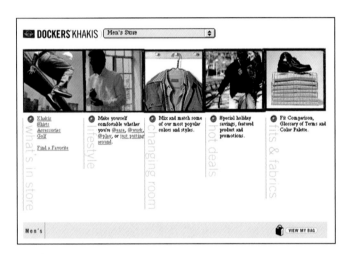

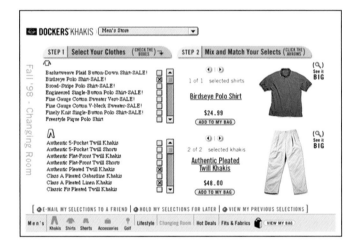

<html>
<head>

<category>	Corporate Image Consumer-Web Sites</head>
<award>	Merit</title>
<agency>	USWeb/CKS/Cupertino
<client>	Levi Strauss and Co.
<url>	www.dockers.com
<art director>	Tim Kain
<writer>	Mary Jeanne Deery
<digital artists>	Hollimarie O'Carroll, Joey Wu
<photographers>	Stewart Ferebee, David Martinez Richard Rethemeyer
<producers>	AnneLise Staal, Traci Cassell, Charl Morkel
<multimedia>	USWeb/CKS
<programmers>	Judi Hengeveld, Aaron Franklin
<creative director>	Mark Frankel
<hardware>	Apple Macintosh, PC
<software>	Adobe AfterEffects, Adobe Illustrator, Adobe ImageReady Adobe Photoshop, Equilibrium Debabelizer Macromedia Fireworks, MS Access, MS SQL Server MS Visual Source Safe, Textpad

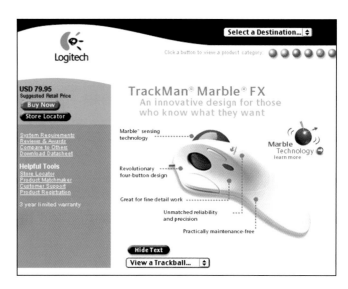

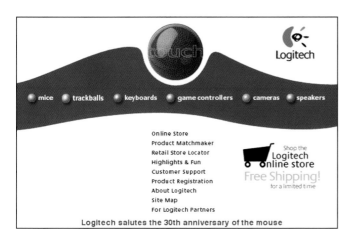

<html>
<head>

<category>	Corporate Image Consumer-Web Sites</head>
<award>	Merit</title>
<agencies>	USWeb/CKS/Cupertino
<client>	Logitech
<url>	www.logitech.com
<art directors>	Jeff Tycz, Hollimarie O'Carroll Bud Northern, Aaron Sagray
<writer>	Sandra Watkins
<digital artists>	Joey Wu, Henry Trieu
<producers>	Martin McGee, Elizabeth Rector
<multimedia>	Tony Rems, Greg O'Bergin, Brad Eaker
<programmers>	Dan Gorman, Nathan Avilla, Blanca Burton Michael Burton, Judi Hengeveld
<creative director>	Mark Frankel
<hardware>	Apple Macintosh PC
<software>	Adobe Illustrator, Adobe Photoshop Macromedia Fireworks

</frameset>
<noframes>

</pageref>
167 <rhp>

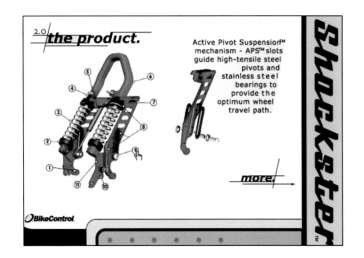

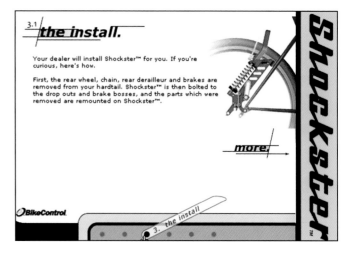

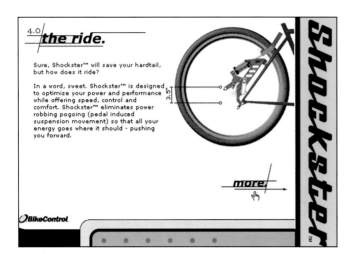

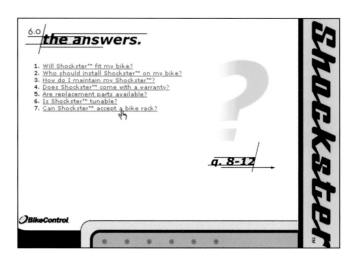

<html>
<head>

<category>	Corporate Image Consumer-Web Sites</head>
<award>	Merit</title>
<agencies>	CyberSight/Portland
<client>	Bike Control
<url>	www.shockster.com
<art director>	Todd Greco
<writer>	Kelly Peters
<producer>	TJ Cathey
<multimedia>	Matt O'Neil
<programmer>	Matt O'Neil
<creative directors>	Kelly Peters Peter Guagenti
<hardware>	Apple Macintosh
<software>	Adobe Illustrator Adobe Photoshop BareBones Edit Macromedia Dreamweaver Macromedia Flash

</frameset>
<noframes>

</pageref>
<168><lhp>

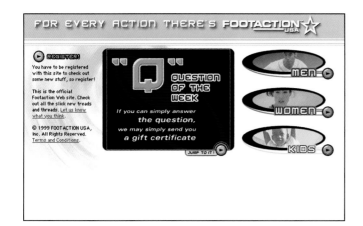

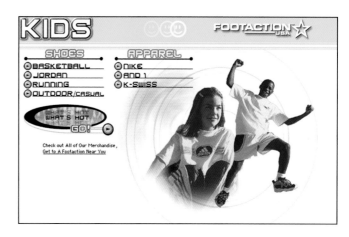

<html>
<head>

<category>	Corporate Image Consumer-Web Sites</head>
<award>	Merit</title>
<agency>	DDB Digital/Dallas
<client>	FootAction USA
<url>	www.footaction.com
<art director>	Troy Harrison
<writer>	Footaction/DDB
<digital artist>	Troy Harrison
<producer>	Kerrey Lucia
<multimedia>	DDB Digital
<programmer>	Dax Phillips
<hardware>	Apple Macintosh
</frameset>	
<noframes>	

	

</pageref>
<169><rhp>

<html>
<head>

<category>	Corporate Image Consumer-Web Sites</head>
<award>	Merit</title>
<agency>	Duffy Design/Minneapolis
<client>	Meow Mix Web Site
<url>	www.meowmix.com
<art directors>	Dan Olson Craig Duffney
<writer>	Debbie Gold
<digital artist>	Mike White
<photographer>	Leslie Fandrich
<producer>	Jennifer Nord
<multimedia>	Mark Sandau
<programmers>	Joe Corbett Mike White
<hardware>	Apple Macintosh
<software>	Adobe Illustrator Adobe Photoshop Macromedia Director

</frameset>
<noframes>

</pageref>
<170><lhp>

<html>
<head>

<category>	Corporate Image Consumer-Web Sites</head>
<award>	Merit</title>
<agency>	Elephant Seven Multimedia/Hamburg
<client>	McKinsey & Company
<url>	www.mckinsey.de
<art director>	Sabine Grammersdorf
<writers>	Sven Mentel Dr. Ulrich Schleith
<programmers>	Jan Boddin Ulf Teege
<creative directors>	Barbara Schmidt Paul Apostolou
<hardware>	Apple Macintosh, PC
<software>	Adobe Photoshop, Allaire Homesite, BBEdit, Macromedia Fireworks

</frameset>
<noframes>

</pageref>
<171><rhp>

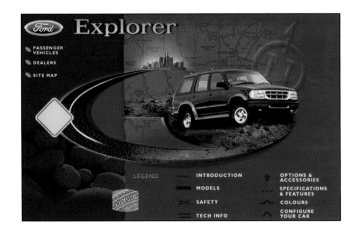
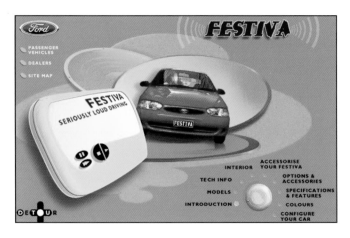
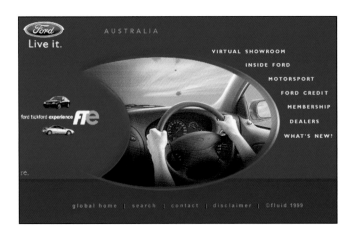

\<html\>
\<head\>

\<category\>	Corporate Image Consumer-Web Sites\</head\>
\<award\>	Merit\</title\>
\<agency\>	Fluid Interactive Communication/North Melbourne
\<client\>	Ford Motor Company of Australia Limited
\<url\>	www.ford.com.au
\<art directors\>	Nick Sayer Damien Royce
\<digital artists\>	Cameron Colson, Boby Nenadovic Lee Mullen, Anhony Gridley
\<photographer\>	Photomation Design and Communication
\<producers\>	Sue McConnell Mandi McPherson
\<multimedia\>	Cameron Colson
\<programmers\>	Travis Winters, Johan Van Zyl Liam Cody, Scott Herskovitz Seb Francis
\<creative director\>	Tania Breberina
\<hardware\>	PC
\<software\>	Adobe Illustrator, Adobe Photoshop Ipix, Macromedia Director, Macromedia Flash Visual Interdex

\</frameset\>
\<noframes\>
\</pageref\>   \<br\>\<br\>
\<br\>\<br\>

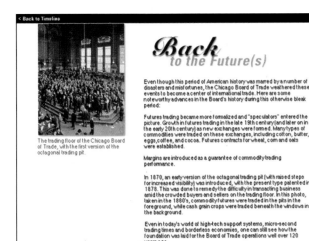

The trading floor of the Chicago Board of Trade, with the first version of the octagonal trading pit.

<html>
<head>

<category>	Corporate Image Consumer-Web Sites</head>
<award>	Merit</title>
<agency>	Laughlin/Constable/Milwaukee
<client>	Chicago Board of Trade
<url>	www.cbot.com/150
<art director>	Elizabeth Morrow-McKenzie
<writer>	Scott Hawk
<digital artist>	Amy Fischer
<producer>	Randy Sprenger
<programmer>	Mark Brenwall
<creative director>	John Constable
<hardware>	Apple Macintosh
<software>	Adobe Illustrator
	Adobe Photoshop
	Gif Builder

</frameset>
<noframes>

</pageref>
<173><rhp>

>

<html>
<head>

<category>	Corporate Image Consumer-Web Sites</head>
<award>	Merit</title>
<agency>	Magnet Interactive/Washington, DC
<client>	Binney & Smith
<url>	www.crayola.com
<art director>	Christina Kenney
<writers>	Lucy Harvey Donna Oetzel Julia Devetski
<producer>	David Wolf
<programmers>	Wendy Jaklitsch Stewart Clatterburgh Myron Wakschlag
<creative directors>	David Belman Mach Arom
<hardware>	Apple Macintosh

</frameset>
<noframes>

</pageref>
<174><lhp>

<html>
<head>

<category>	Corporate Image Consumer-Web Sites</head>
<award>	Merit</title>
<agency>	Magnet Interactive/Washington, DC
<client>	Nissan Motor Corp USA
<url>	www.nissan-usa.com
<art director>	Anthony Monohan
<writers>	Freddy Nager Julia Devetski
<digital artist>	Helen Yang
<producer>	Stacy Burgum
<programmers>	Happy Tsugawa Thomas Deaton Samuel Goldstein Mike Rosenberg
<hardware>	Apple Macintosh

</frameset>
<noframes>

</pageref>
<175><rhp>

<html>
<head>

<category>	Corporate Image Consumer-Web Sites</head>
<award>	Merit</title>
<agency>	Quantum Leap Communications/Chicago
<client>	American Airlines
<url>	www.aa.com
<art director>	David Hernandez
<writer>	Peter Giovagnoli
<digital artists>	Margo Johnson Philip Machalski Mark Hines Michael Forsythe
<producers>	Matthew Hanson Sue Kehias Debra Bean
<programmer>	Michael Oltman
<creative director>	Richard Guiliani
<hardware>	UNIX
<software>	Adobe After Effects, Adobe Illustrator Adobe Photoshop, Allaire Homesite, BBEdit Equilibrium Debabelizer, GifBuilder

</frameset>
<noframes>

</pageref>

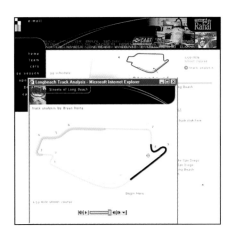

<html>
<head>

<category>	Corporate Image Consumer-Web Sites</head>
<award>	Merit</title>
<agency>	Resource Marketing/Columbus
<client>	Team Rahal
<url>	www.rahal.com
<art director>	Todd Yuzwa
<writer>	Doug Burdick
<digital artists>	Courtney Jones Mark Robinson Michael Polivka
<photographer>	Paul Webb
<producer>	Andrew Bornand
<programmers>	Andrew Clute Jean-Marx Mantilla
<creative director>	Doug Burdick
<hardware>	Apple Macintosh PC
<software>	Adobe ImageReady Adobe Photoshop Macromedia SoundEdit Quicktime VR

</frameset>
<noframes>

</pageref>
177 <rhp>

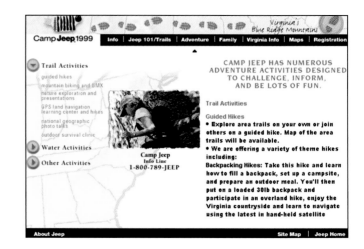

`<html>`
`<head>`

`<category>`	Corporate Image Consumer-Web Sites`</head>`
`<award>`	Merit`</title>`
`<agency>`	Ross Roy Communications/Bloomfield Hills
`<client>`	DaimlerChrysler
`<url>`	www.jeepunpaved.com
`<art directors>`	Marie deVera Seiden, Carl Cuchetti
`<writer>`	Brendan Rohan
`<digital artists>`	Buffington & Associates, Andy Czilok Digital Image
`<photographers>`	Dave Scheich, Tom Burkhart Peggy Day, Paul Primeau
`<producer>`	C. Leigh Hollar
`<multimedia>`	Bob Kuck, Gale George, Patrick Burnside Libby Saelzler
`<programmers>`	Jim Jonah, Nathan Wray, Michael Howard
`<creative directors>`	John J. Keenan, Jr., Lydia Porter Latocki
`<hardware>`	Apple Macintosh, PC
`<software>`	Adobe ImageReady, Adobe Photoshop BBEdit, Quicktime VR Studio

`</frameset>`
`<noframes>`
`<br><br>`
`</pageref>`
`<178><lhp>`
`<br><br>`

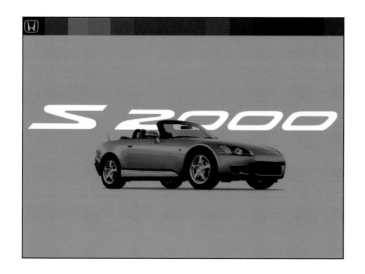

Passport 4WD LX shown in Ebony Black.

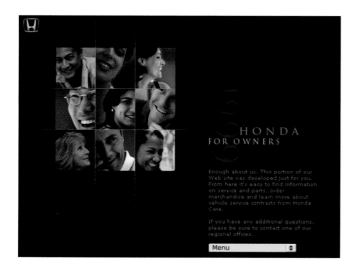

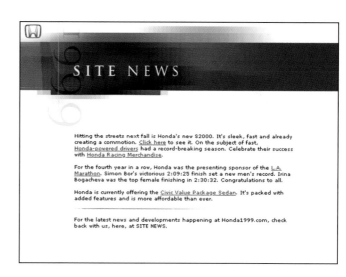

<html>
<head>

<category>	Corporate Image Consumer-Web Sites</head>
<award>	Merit</title>
<agency>	Rubin Postaer Interactive/Santa Monica
<client>	American Honda Motor Co.
<url>	www.honda1999.com
<art director>	Bang Pham
<writers>	Claudia Saunders Dan Roberts J. Barbush
<digital artist>	Laurie Slaven
<producers>	Michael Sterner Julie Johnson
<programmer>	Jeff Kwong
<creative director>	Tom Roberts
<hardware>	Apple Macintosh

</frameset>
<noframes>

</pageref>
<179><rhp>

<html>
<head>

\<category>	Corporate Image Consumer-Web Sites\</head>
\<award>	Merit\</title>
\<agency>	Sapient/Studio Archetype/San Francisco
\<client>	Discovery Communications
\<url>	www.travelchannel.com
\<art director>	Paula Meiselman
\<writers>	Natasha Banta Rachel Bernstein Linda Yeo
\<producers>	Mary Tang Wendy Smith
\<multimedia>	Paul Wang, Nancy Ordover Kara Nickols
\<programmers>	Zach Baum Matt Hergert
\<creative director>	Brian Forst
\<hardware>	Apple Macintosh
\<software>	Adobe Illustrator, Adobe Photoshop

<html>
<head>

<category>	Corporate Image Consumer-Web Sites</head>
<award>	Merit</title>
<agency>	Siegel & Gale/New York
<client>	Kodak
<url>	www.kodak.com/go/further
<art director>	Holly Lau
<digital artists>	Andreas Euler Marcelo Mijares Karen Tan
<producers>	Carolyn Dobbs Michael Kroll Don Chanfrau Steve Pollack
<programmers>	Jim Tuite Karon Jones Noah Mitman
<hardware>	Apple Macintosh

</frameset>
<noframes>

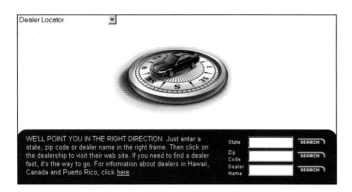

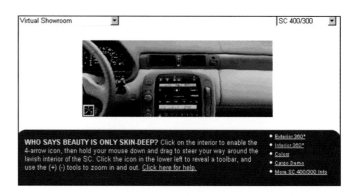

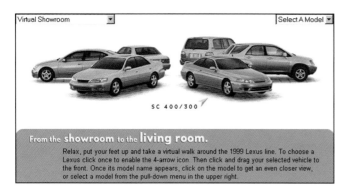

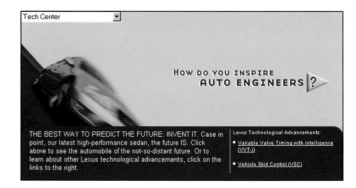

<html>
<head>

<category>	Corporate Image Consumer-Web Sites</head>
<award>	Merit</title>
<agency>	Team One Advertising/El Segundo
<client>	Lexus
<url>	www.lexus.com
<art directors>	Michael Takeshita, Brian Doyle, Courtenay Thomas
<writers>	Scott Ivener, Beau Elwell, Nancy Nelms
<digital artists>	Darren Chang, Lawrence Matthews
<photographer>	Rick Rusing
<producers>	Francesca Cohn, Dara Dellinger, Sandy Eifert
<multimedia>	USI
<creative directors>	Gabrielle Mayeur, Tom Cordner
<hardware>	Apple Macintosh, PC
<software>	Active Server Pages, Adobe Illustrator Adobe Photoshop, Macromedia Flash

</frameset>
</pageref>   <noframes>
<182><lhp>

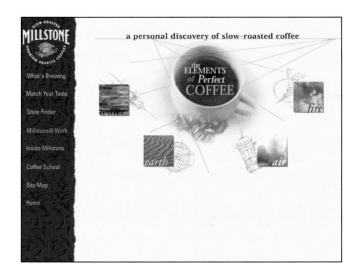

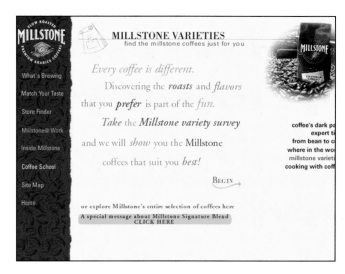

\<html\>
\<head\>

\<category\>	Corporate Image Consumer-Web Sites\</head\>
\<award\>	Merit\</title\>
\<agency\>	Think New Ideas/Los Angeles
\<client\>	Millstone Coffee
\<url\>	www.millstone.com
\<art directors\>	Carolyn Clendenning, Joe Suarez
\<writer\>	John Murphy
\<digital artists\>	Carolyn Clendenning Christine Fernandez Jenny Woo
\<producer\>	Jim Bixler
\<multimedia\>	Think New Ideas
\<programmers\>	Mike Petry, Alec Cove
\<creative director\>	Brian Martin
\<hardware\>	Apple Macintosh
\<software\>	Adobe Illustrator, Adobe Photoshop BBEdit, Macromedia Flash

\</frameset\>
\<noframes\>
\<br\>\<br\>

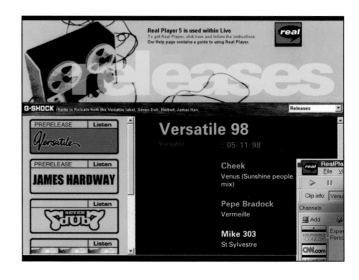

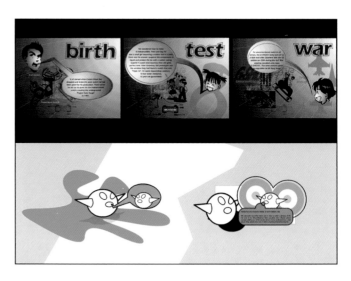

`<html>`
`<head>`

`<category>`	Corporate Image Consumer-Web Sites`</head>`
`<award>`	Merit`</title>`
`<agency>`	Travis Sully Harari/London
`<client>`	Casio G-Shock
`<url>`	www.g-club.net
`<art director>`	Paul Thurlow
`<writer>`	Emma E. Forrest
`<digital artists>`	Paul Thurlow Rowan Allinson Amo Bassan
`<producer>`	Cecile Ferre
`<programmer>`	Nathan Carr
`<hardware>`	Linux Box Server
`<software>`	Apache, Macromedia Flash MySQL Database, RealPlayer

`</frameset>`
`<noframes>`
`<br><br>`

`</pageref>`
`<184<lhp>`
`<br><br>`

<html>
<head>

<category>	Corporate Image Consumer-Web Sites</head>
<award>	Merit</title>
<agency>	US Interactive/New York
<client>	Network Solutions
<url>	www.worldnic.com
<writer>	Dave Keener
<digital artist>	Neil Bar-or
<producer>	Josh Unger
<creative director>	Bronson Smith
<hardware>	Apple Macintosh
<software>	Adobe Illustrator Adobe Photoshop

</frameset>
<noframes>

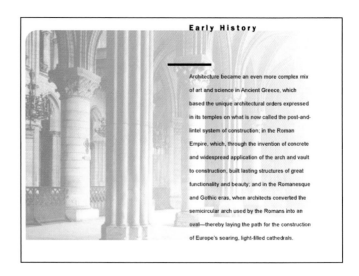

<html>
<head>

<category>	Corporate Image Consumer-Web Sites</head>
<award>	Merit</title>
<agency>	USWeb/CKS/San Francisco
<client>	Janus Mutual Funds
<url>	www.Janus.com
<writers>	Tracy Cohen, Tina Andropoulos Mark McCormick, Leslie Rule
<illustrator>	Michael Lenahan
<digital artists>	Michael Lenahan, Doug Muse Maureen Agius
<producers>	Lisa Grzesiek Yiannis Psaroudis
<multimedia>	Pete Howells
<programmers>	Dave Cronin, Ryan Shaw, Pam Miklaski Sasha Panasik, Kristine Gual, John Adair
<creative director>	Eric Johnson
<hardware>	Apple Macintosh

</frameset>
</pageref>   <noframes>
<186><lhp>

<html>
<head>

<category>	Corporate Image Consumer-Web Sites</head>
<award>	Merit</title>
<agency>	USWeb/CKS/San Francisco
<client>	Toyota Motor Europe
<url>	www.lexus-europe.com
<art director>	Michael Lenahan
<writer>	Tracy Cohen
<illustrator>	Loc Ho
<digital artists>	Loc Ho Jens Sonnenchein Mark Stockwell
<producers>	Ryan Currier, Annette Greif
<programmers>	John Adair, Pao-Lin Hsu, Pam Miklaski
<creative director>	Eric Johnson
<hardware>	Apple Macintosh, PC
<software>	Adobe Illustrator, Adobe Photoshop, Allaire Cold Fusion, Allaire Homesite, BBEdit, Claris FileMaker Pro, Equilibrium Debabelizer, Java Plugins, LivePicture Studio

</frameset>
<noframes>

</pageref>
187<rhp>

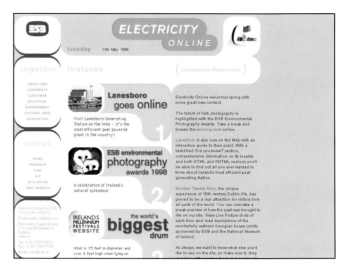

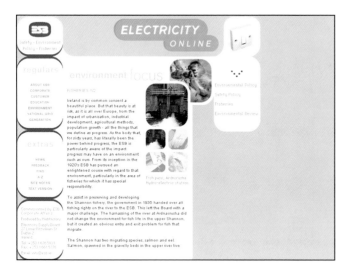

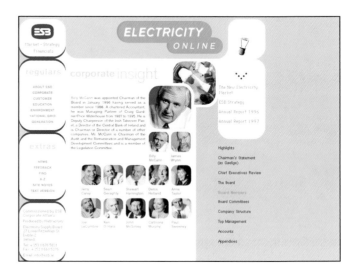

`<html>`
`<head>`

`<category>`	Corporate Image Consumer-Web Sites`</head>`
`<award>`	Merit`</title>`
`<agency>`	Webfactory/Dublin
`<client>`	ESB
`<url>`	www.esb.ie
`<art director>`	Marcus Lynam
`<writer>`	Catherine Feeney
`<digital artist>`	Richard Pittham
`<producer>`	Simon Walsh
`<multimedia>`	Webfactory
`<programmers>`	Niall Colgan, Brendan McNally
`<hardware>`	Apple Macintosh, PC
`<software>`	Adobe AfterEffects, Adobe Illustrator, Adobe ImageReady Adobe Photoshop, Adobe Premier Equilibrium DeBabelizer, Live Picture, Macromedia Dreamweaver Macromedia Fireworks, Macromedia Freehand, Macromedia SoundEdit, Quicktime Specular Infini-D

`</frameset>`
`</pageref>`   `<noframes>`

<html>
<head>

<category>	Corporate Image Consumer-CD-ROM</head>
<award>	Merit</title>
<agency>	adidas International/Portland
<client>	adidas International Basketball Communications
<art director>	Hein Haugland
<writers>	Andrews Jenkins, Devin Moore
<digital artists>	adidas International Designworks/USA
<producers>	adidas International Designworks/USA
<multimedia>	Joe Meade
<photographers>	Pablo Aguilar, Steve Bonini
<programmer>	Designworks/USA
<creative director>	Kadie Casey
<hardware>	Apple Macintosh
<software>	Adobe Photoshop, Adobe Premiere, Macromedia Director Macromedia SoundEdit 16, Media 100, Quicktime

</frameset>
<noframes>

</pageref>
189<rhp>

\<html>
\<head>

\<category>	Corporate Image Consumer-CD-ROM\</head>
\<award>	Merit\</title>
\<agency>	BrandGames/New York
\<client>	General Mills
\<art director>	Jason Shenkman
\<writer>	Scott Randall
\<illustrators>	Kyle Vannoy, Jason Vaughn Anthony Pereira, Robert Santiago Jason Shenkman
\<digital artists>	John Sousa, Marc Tattersall Kyle Vannoy, Jason Vaughn James Orsi, Eddy Wang
\<producers>	Scott Randall Mike Taramykin
\<multimedia>	Tony Rems, Greg O'Bergin Brad Eaker
\<programmer>	Tom Kirchner
\<creative director>	Mike Taramykin
\<hardware>	PC
\<software>	3-D studio max, Adobe Photoshop, Animator Pro AXA Animation Software, Pro Tools

\</frameset>

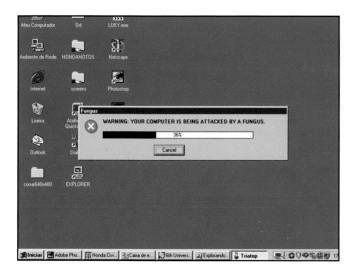

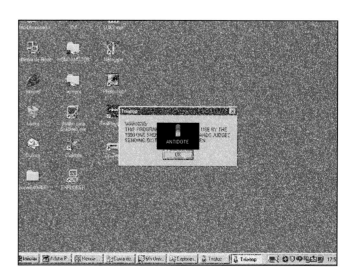

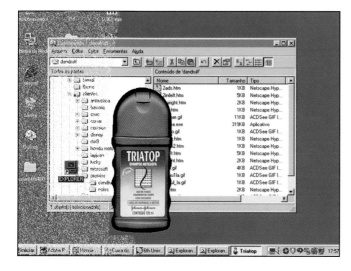

<html>
<head>

<category>	Corporate Image Consumer-Other Digital Advertising</head>
<award>	Merit</title>
<agency>	DM9DDB Publicidade/São Paulo
<client>	Johnson & Johnson
<url>	www.dm9.com.br/oneshow
<art director>	Eugenio Duarte
<writer>	PJ Pereira
<producer>	Zeno Millet
<multimedia>	Webra
<creative director>	Tomas Lorente
<hardware>	PC
<software>	Delphi

</frameset>
<noframes>

</pageref>
<191><rhp>

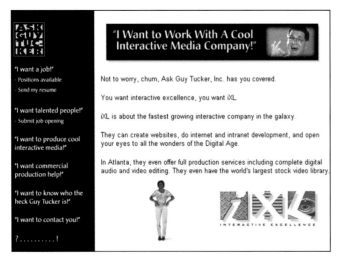

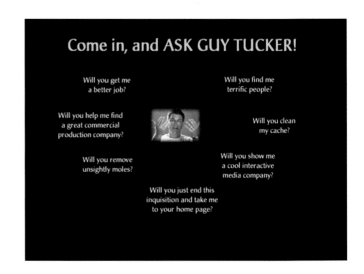

<html>
<head>

<category>	Corporate Image Business to Business-Web Sites</head>
<award>	Merit</title>
<agency>	Ask Guy Tucker/Atlanta
<client>	Ask Guy Tucker
<url>	www.askguy.com
<art director>	Juan Pablo Gnecco/StudioCom
<writers>	Patrick Scullin/Ames Scullin O'Haire
<digital artists>	Juan Pablo Gnecco, Deepali Gokhale
<photographer>	Juan Pablo Gnecco
<producer>	Juan Pablo Gnecco
<multimedia>	StudioCom
<programmer>	Juan Pablo Gnecco
<creative directors>	Guy Tucker, Juan Pablo Gnecco,Patrick Scullin
<hardware>	Power Macintosh, FireMax Video Card Cannon Optura DV Camera, Wacom Tablet
<software>	Adobe AfterEffects, Adobe PageMill, Adobe Photoshop Adobe Premiere, #2 Pencil with eraser

</pageref>
192<lhp>

</frameset>
<noframes>

<head>
<category>Corporate Image Business to Buisness-Web Sites</head>

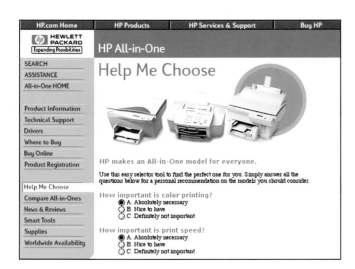

<html>
<head>

<category>	Corporate Image Business to Business-Web Sites </head>
<award>	Merit</title>
<agency>	AGENCY.COM/Chicago
<client>	Hewlett-Packard
<url>	www.all-in-one-home.com
<art director>	Dan Rehmann
<writer>	Mark Scantlebury
<photographer>	Todd Eckleman
<producer >	Jana Geary
<multimedia >	Mark Scantlebury
<programmers>	Jason Wells
	Andy Scasso
	John Croft
<creative director>	Joe Parker
<hardware>	Apple Macintosh, PC
<software>	Adobe Illustrator, Adobe Photoshop
	Allaire Homesite, Equilibrium Debabelizer
	Macromedia Director

</frameset>
<noframes>

</pageref>
<193><rhp>

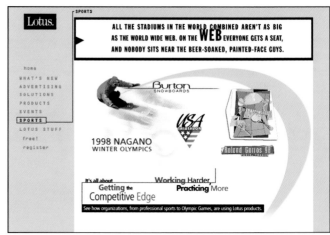

<html>
<head>

<category>	Corporate Image Business to Business-Web Sites</head>
<award>	Merit</title>
<agency>	Hill Holliday Interactive/Boston
<client>	Lotus
<url>	www.lotus.com/programs/workthewebad.nsf
<art director>	Dmitri Cavander
<writers>	Vashti Brotherhood Jim Milke
<programmers>	Matt Denault Stacey Duda Raj Khanna Scott Olivieri Tariq Qureshi
<hardware>	Apple Macintosh
<software>	Adobe Illustrator Adobe Photoshop Equilibrium Debabelizer Gif Builder Lotus Avian Streaming Media Lotus Domino Lotus Notes

</frameset>
<noframes>
</pageref>

<194><lhp>

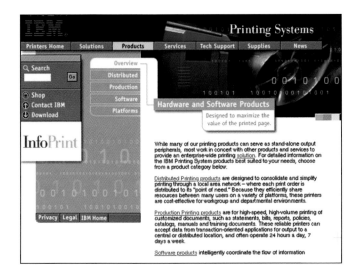

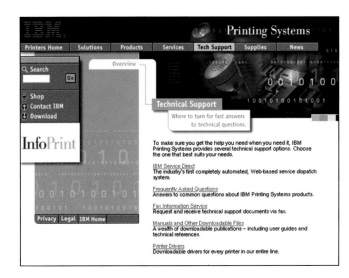

<html>
<head>

<category>	Corporate Image Business to Business-Web Sites</head>
<award>	Merit</title>
<agency>	Ogilvy Interactive/New York
<client>	IBM
<url>	www.oandmi.com/ibm/printers/
<art director>	Warren Kemp
<writer>	Scott Storrs
<producer>	Janet Heettner
<creative director>	Jan Leth
<hardware>	Apple Macintosh
<software>	Adobe Illustrator
	Adobe Photoshop

</frameset>
<noframes>

</pageref>
<195><rhp>

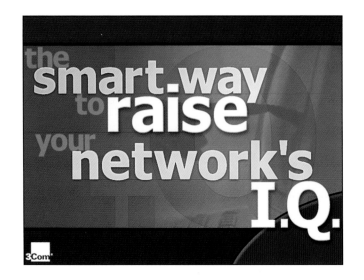
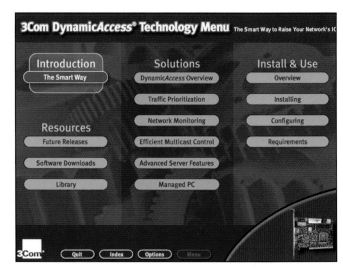

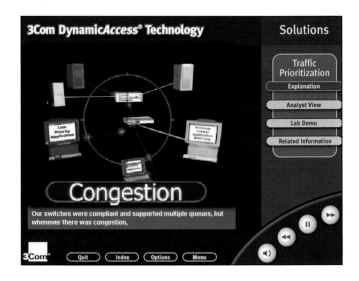

\<html>
\<head>

\<category>	Corporate Image Business to Business-CD-ROM\</head>
\<award>	Merit\</title>
\<agency>	E.ON Interactive/Santa Cruz
\<client>	3Com
\<art director>	Tim Levy
\<writers>	Paul Harris Chris Finnie
\<producer>	Adam J. Fleischer
\<multimedia>	Andrew Webster
\<programmer>	Joseph Krilanovich
\<hardware>	Apple Macintosh, PC
\<software>	Adobe Illustrator Adobe Photoshop Macromedia Director Macromedia SoundEdit 16 Movie Cleaner Pro

\</frameset>
\<noframes>
\</pageref>   \
\

\
\

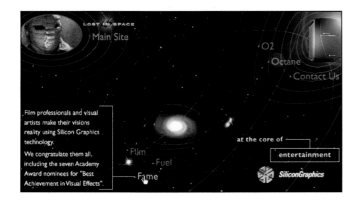
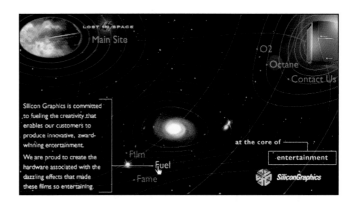
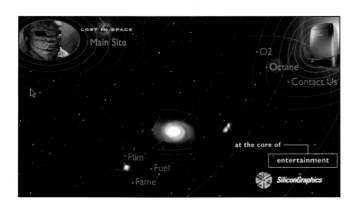
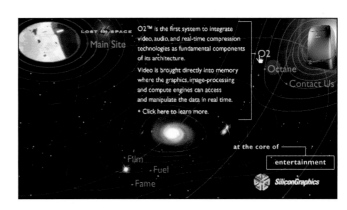

<html>
<head>

<category>	Corporate Image-Other Digital Advertising</head>
<award>	Merit</title>
<agency>	USWeb/CKS/Cupertino
<client>	Silicon Graphics
<art director>	Tom Walter
<writer>	John Avilla
<programmer>	Judi Hengeveld
<creative directors>	John Avilla Mark Frankel
<hardware>	Apple Macintosh PC SGI
<software>	Adobe Illustrator Adobe Photoshop Textpad Html

</frameset>
<noframes>

>

</pageref>
<197><rhp>

WELCOME TO
patagonia®

Quality Outdoor Clothing and Gear Since 1973

online store   patagonia.com

Photo: CHARLIE MUNSEY

<html>
<head>

<category>	Direct Marketing-Web Sites</head>
<award>	Merit</title>
<agency>	ADJACENCY/San Francisco
<client>	Patagonia
<url>	www.patagonia.com
<art directors>	Bernie DeChant Andrew Sather
<writer>	Betsy Haygood
<digital artists>	Pete Petras Bernie DeChant Mike Lin
<producers>	Leni Litonjua, Jen Wolf Sondra Russell, Pascal
<programmers>	Carlo Calica, Matt Kirchstein Anton Prastowo
<creative director>	Andrew Sather
<hardware>	Apple Macintosh
<software>	Adobe Illustrator Adobe Photoshop, BBEdit

</frameset>
<noframes>
</pageref>
<198><lhp>

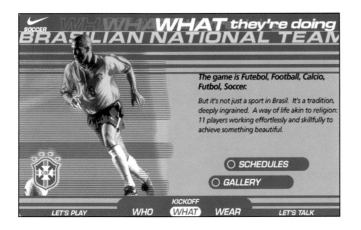

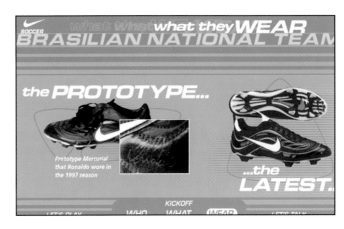

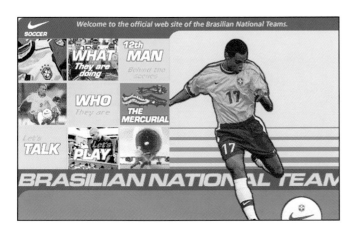

\<html>
\<head>

\<category>	Direct Marketing-Web Sites\</head>
\<award>	Merit\</title>
\<agency>	AGENCY.COM/New York
\<client>	Nike
\<url>	www.brasilfutebol.com
\<art director>	Tim Carrier
\<writer>	Tim Doherty
\<digital artists>	Heidi Stephens Min Chang
\<producers>	Chad Ruble Kim Albert
\<programmers>	Mike Parker, Vicky Chui
\<creative directors>	Deanne Draeger Andrew Leitch
\<hardware>	Apple Macintosh
\<software>	Adobe Illustrator Adobe ImageReady Adobe Photoshop BBEdit Macromedia Flash

\</frameset>
\<noframes>
\
\

`<html>`
`<head>`

`<category>`	Direct Marketing-Web Sites`</head>`
`<award>`	Merit`</title>`
`<agency>`	Digital Pulp/New York
`<client>`	egghead.com
`<url>`	www.egghead.com
`<art director>`	Chris Barrett
`<producer>`	Gene Lewis
`<programmers>`	Justin Blecker Alan Guttman
`<creative director>`	Bruce Goodman
`<hardware>`	Apple Macintosh, PC
`<software>`	Adobe ImageReady, Adobe Illustrator Adobe Photoshop, Allaire Homesite Bare Bone BBEdit, Equilibrium Debabelizer Gif Builder, HTML Production, Mapper
`</frameset>`	
`<noframes>`	
`  `	

<html>
<head>

<category>	Direct Marketing-Web Sites</head>
<award>	Merit</title>
<agency>	Organic Online/San Francisco
<client>	Corbis
<url>	store.corbis.com
<art directors>	Fanny Krivoy, Sara Golding
<writer>	Carol Lane
<digital artists>	Jonathan Hills Ray Mancini
<producers>	Alexis Hasiotis Jennifer Steele Josh Goldberg
<programmers>	Tim Howland Patrick Snell Vivian Chang Kefan Xu John McCaughey Gary Roth
<creative director>	Paul Krygowski
<hardware>	NT Server, Backup Server Local Director Machine
<software>	Windows NT IIS SQL Server Site Server 3.0 Commerce Server Edition Transaction Server

</frameset>
<noframes>

</pageref>
<201><rhp>

\<html\>
\<head\>

\<category\>	Direct Marketing-Web Sites\</head\>
\<award\>	Merit\</title\>
\<agency\>	Organic Online/San Francisco
\<client\>	Starbucks Coffee Company
\<url\>	www.starbucks.com
\<art directors\>	Nancy Pinney, Marusa Debrini
\<writer\>	Jenny Hanna
\<digital artists\>	Patrick Farley, Mark Levinson, Tracey Limon Jeffrey Reid, Deborah Smith
\<producers\>	Kerry Fitzgerald, Leland Rechis Heidi Wells, Paul Blair
\<programmers\>	Tony Pierce, Ed Bean, Chris Maresca Shelila Wakida, Ray Hunter
\<creative directors\>	Michael Cory, Sara Ortloff
\<hardware\>	SQL Server
\<software\>	Microsoft 2S, Active Server Pages Site Server Commerce Edition, Visual InterDev

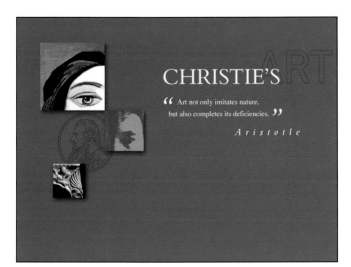

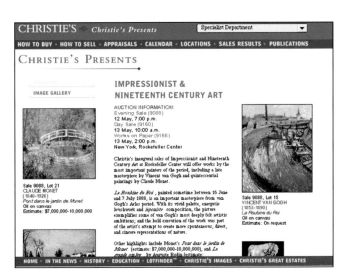

<html>
<head>

<category>	Direct Marketing-Web Sites</head>
<award>	Merit</title>
<agency>	Razorfish/New York
<client>	Christie's
<url>	www.christies.com
<art director>	Thomas Mueller
<digital artist>	Thomas Mueller
<producer>	Brandi Gil
<programmers>	Jason Jeffries Aaron Berkson
<creative director>	Craig Vanarick
<hardware>	Apple Macintosh PC
<software>	Adobe Illustrator Adobe Photoshop

</frameset>
<noframes>

OxfordExpress

Your perfect dress shirt is just a few clicks away.

We offer a lot of dress shirts. With all the combinations of fabrics, patterns, collar types, colors and cuts, we have over 10,000 shirts in our warehouse! To make sense of them all, we've developed Oxford Express. It gives you a sense of **every** dress shirt that's available. But at the same time, it helps you identify **your perfect shirt** with just a few steps.

We're really excited about Oxford Express. Give it a try... and then tell us if you find it as helpful as we think you will.

All Shirts
Explore the possibilities

White Buttondown
Just choose size and cut

Blue Buttondown
Just choose size and cut

Oxford Express gives you smart access to the complete inventory of Lands' End tailored shirts -- but it may take a while to download over slow modem connections. Below are estimates of how long it may take for your computer to load Oxford Express:

T1: about 15 seconds
ISDN: about 1 minute
56K modem: about 1 minute 30 seconds
33.6 modem: about 2 minutes 15 seconds
28.8 modem: about 2 minutes 45 seconds
14.4 modem: about 5 minutes 30 seconds

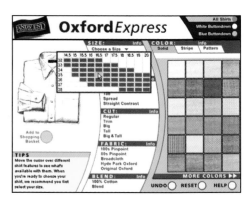

\<html\>
\<head\>

\<category\>	Direct Marketing-Web Sites\</head\>
\<award\>	Merit\</title\>
\<agency\>	Red Sky Interactive/San Francisco
\<client\>	Lands' End
\<url\>	www.landsend.com
\<art director\>	Genevieve Moore
\<digital artist\>	Divya Srinivasan
\<producers\>	Jill Lefkowitz, Jessica Burdman, Andrew Klein
\<multimedia\>	Red Sky Interactive
\<programmers\>	Marc Blanchard, Adam Kane, Matt McGlincy Gretchen Atwood, Andrea Gallagher Sophie Jasson-Holt, Yelena Glezer
\<creative director\>	Genevieve Moore
\<hardware\>	Apple Macintosh PC
\<software\>	Adobe Photoshop, Director Fireworks, Java Microsoft Visual Studio, ModaCAD, ModaCATALOG

\</frameset\>
\<noframes\>
\<br\>\<br\>

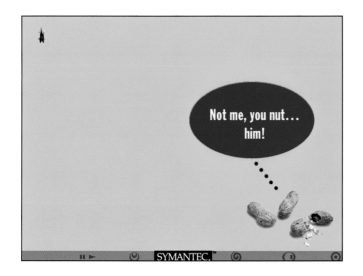

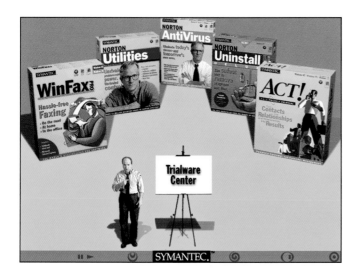

<html>
<head>

<category>	Direct Marketing-CD-ROM</head>
<award>	Merit</title>
<agency>	Medius IV/San Francisco
<client>	Symantec Corporation
<art director>	Shirley Rafieetary
<writers>	Susan Carp, Julie Marcus
<digital artist>	Fred Lewis
<producer>	Jeanne Brophy
<multimedia>	Medius IV
<programmers>	Ted Jones, Slav Kasyanov
<creative director>	Moez Rafieetary
<hardware>	PC, PowerMac
<software>	Adobe Premiere Adobe Illustrator Adobe Photoshop Equilibrium DeBabelizer Macromedia Director

</frameset>
<noframes>

</pageref>
<205><rhp>

<html>
<head>

<category>	Integrated Branding Campaign</head>
<award>	Merit</title>
<agency>	APL Digital/New York
<client>	Iridium
<url>	www.iridium.com
<software>	Netscape Enterprise Oracle/PL/SQL

</frameset>
<noframes>

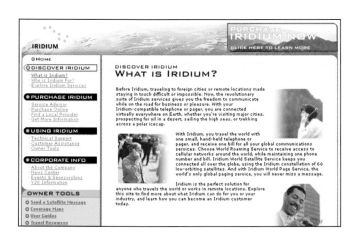 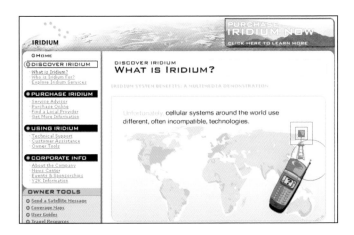

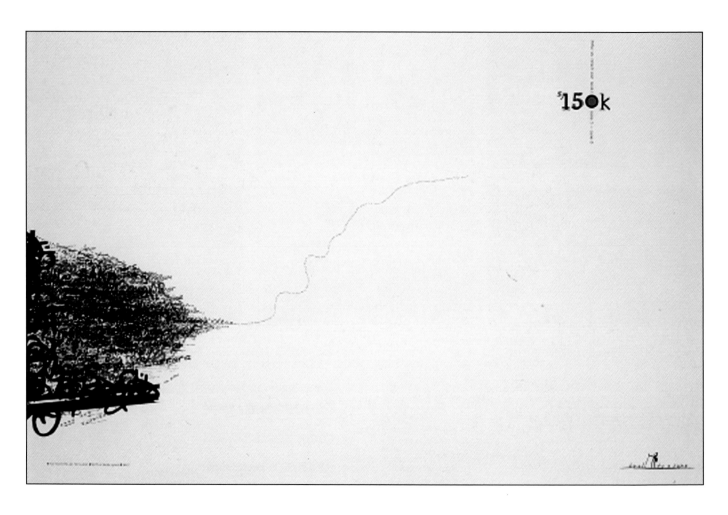

'15●k

>

<html>
<head>

<category>	Integrated Branding Campaign</head>
<award>	Merit</title>
<agency>	Hill Holliday Interactive/Boston
<client>	Trail to a Cure
<url>	trailtoacure.hhcc.com
<art director>	Murat Bodur
<writer>	Vashti Brotherhood
<illustrators>	Murat Bodur
	Juan Pedro Di Polo
<programmers>	Scott Olivieri
	Mike Jeffers
<hardware>	Apple Macintosh
<software>	Adobe Illustrator
	Adobe Photoshop Equilibrium
	Debabelizer
	GifBuilder
	Lotus Avian Streaming Media
	Lotus Domino
	Lotus Notes

</frameset>
<noframes>

</pageref>
<208><lhp>

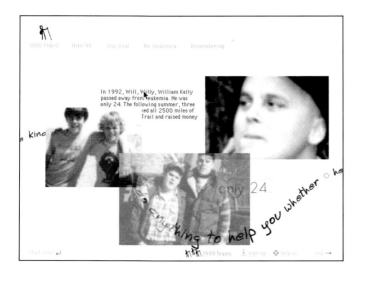
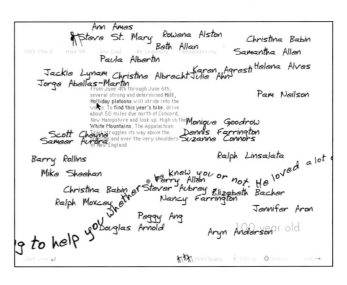

</pageref>
<209><rhp>

<html>
<head>

<category>	Integrated Branding Campaign</head>
<award>	Merit</title>
<agency>	Magnet Interactive/Washington, DC
<client>	Kellogg Company
<url>	www.tonythetiger.com
<art director>	William Colgrave
<writer>	Michael Grau
<producers>	Derek Cicero David Wolf
<creative director>	David Belman

</frameset>
<noframes>
</pageref>

<210><lhp>

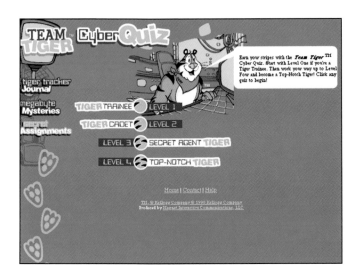

</pageref>
<211><rhp>

<html>
<head>

<category>	</head>
<award>	Merit</title>
<agency>	Messner Vetere Berger McNamee Schmetterer/Euro RSCG/New York
<client>	Philips Electronics
<hardware>	Apple Macintosh
<software>	Adobe Illustrator Adobe Photoshop Macromedia Flash

</frameset>
<noframes>

</pageref>
<212><lhp>

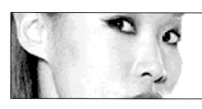

I don't worry about the *future.*

PHILIPS

I carry it in my *pocket.*

PHILIPS

I carry it in my *pocket.*

PHILIPS

I carry it in my *pocket.*

PHILIPS

Home Cinema
Collection

Communications
Collection

Display
Collection

CD Technologies
Collection

PC Business
Collection

Product Search

TV the way it should be! This 64"
TV is a fully integrated, high definition
digital TV, with Dolby Ditigal™ sound
in a widescreen format. The picture
performance, driven by three 9" CRTs,
is the brightest and most detailed ever.

64" (diagonal) HDTV

PHILIPS
Let's make things better

</pageref>
<213><rhp>

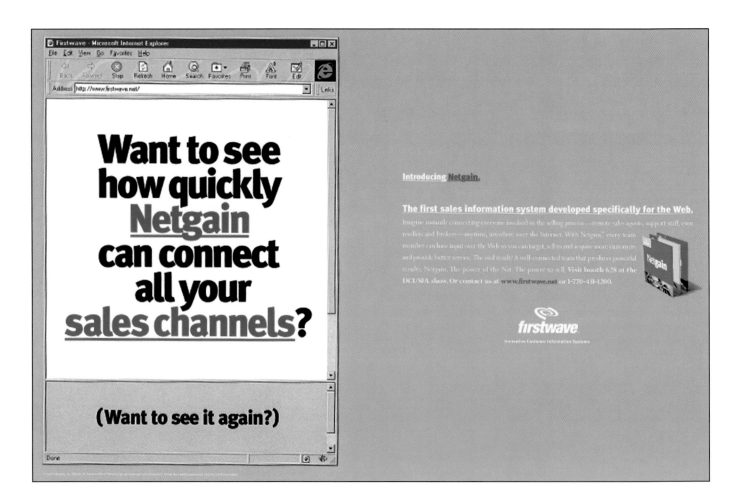

<html>
<head>

<category>	Integrated Branding Campaign</head>
<award>	Merit</title>
<agency>	Sicola Martin/Austin
<client>	Firstwave Technologies, Inc.
<url>	awards.sicolamartin.com
<hardware>	Apple Macintosh PC
<software>	Adobe Illustrator Adobe Photoshop BareBones BBEdit Microsoft Frontpage98 Microsoft Visual Interdev

</frameset>
<noframes>

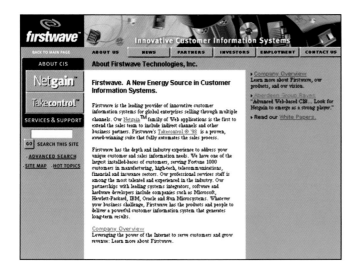

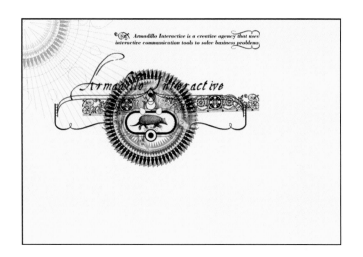

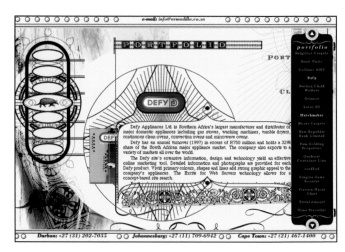

\>

\<html\>
\<head\>

\<category\>	Self-Promotion-Web Sites\</head\>
\<award\>	Merit\</title\>
\<agency\>	Armadillo Interactive/Durban
\<client\>	Armadillo Interactive
\<url\>	www.armadillo.co.za
\<art director\>	Stephen Embleton
\<writers\>	Kerry Somers Jacques van Schoor
\<producers\>	Duncan Forrest David Burstein
\<programmer\>	Scott Dukes
\<creative director\>	Stephen Embleton
\<hardware\>	Apple Macintosh PC
\<software\>	Adobe Photoshop Macromedia Freehand

\</frameset\>
\<noframes\>
\<br\>\<br\>

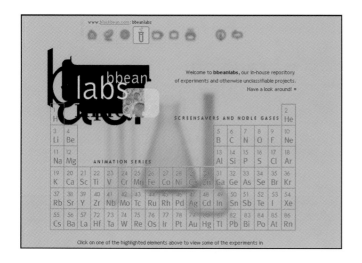

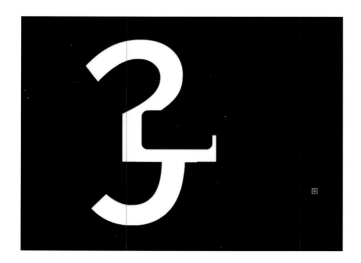

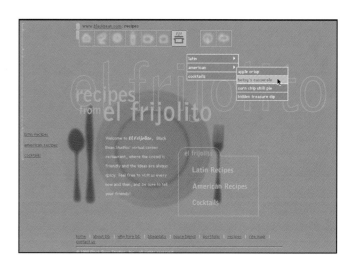

<html>
<head>

<category>	Self-Promotion-Web Sites</head>
<award>	Merit</title>
<agency>	Black Bean Studios/Boston
<client>	Black Bean Studios
<url>	www.blackbean.com
<art directors>	Claudio Luis Vera, Alisha Haydn Vera Jodi Vautrin
<writers>	Claudio Luis Vera Sarah Allen
<producers>	Sarah Allen Judy Wong
<multimedia>	Black Bean Studios
<programmers>	Jason Giaconne, Judy Wong Sarah Allen, Claudio Luis Vera Dave Bernick
<hardware>	Apple Macintosh, PC
<software>	Adobe Illustrator Adobe ImageReady Adobe Photoshop

</frameset>
<noframes>

</pageref>
217<rhp>

<html>
<head>

<category>	Self-Promotion-Web Sites</head>
<award>	Merit</title>
<agency>	C3 Incorporated/New York
<client>	C3 Incorporated
<url>	www.c3inc.com
<writer>	Billie Harber
<programmers>	Chris Rauch Richard Madigan
<creative director>	Randall Hensley
<hardware>	Apple Macintosh Unix
<software>	Adobe Illustrator Adobe Photoshop BBEdit Macromedia Director Macromedia Flash

</frameset>
<noframes>

</pageref>
<218><lhp>

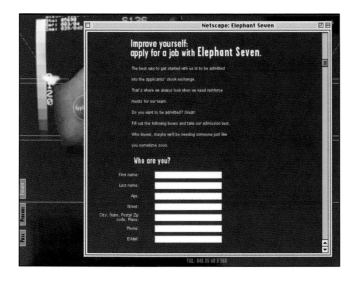

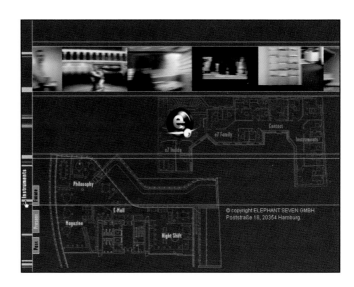

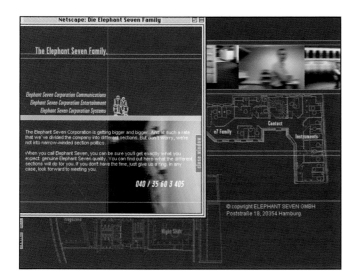

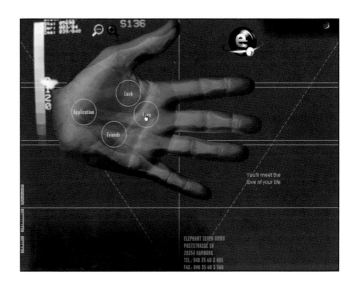

\<html\>
\<head\>

\<category\>	Self-Promotion-Web Sites\</head\>
\<award\>	Merit\</title\>
\<agency\>	Elephant Seven Multimedia/Hamburg
\<client\>	Elephant Seven Multimedia
\<url\>	www.e-7.com
\<art directors\>	Sabine Grammersdorf Andreas Henkel
\<writers\>	Christian Binnewies Sven Mentel Maurice Morell
\<programmers\>	Jan Boddin Thomas Hicks
\<creative directors\>	Barbara Schmidt Paul Apostolou
\<hardware\>	Apple Macintosh, PC
\<software\>	Adobe Photoshop, Allaire Homesite BBEdit, Director Fireworks

\</frameset\>
\<noframes\>
\<br\>\<br\>

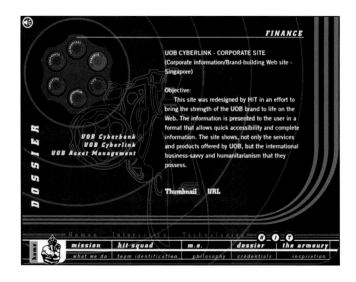

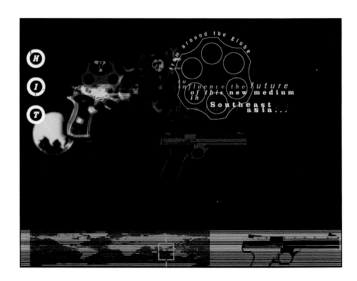

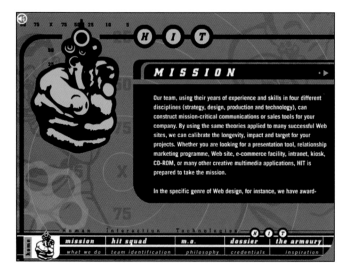

<html>
<head>

<category>	Self-Promotion-Web Sites</head>
<award>	Merit</title>
<agency>	Human Interaction Technologies (HIT)/Singapore
<client>	Human Interaction Technologies (HIT)
<url>	www.hit.com.sg
<art director>	Roy Salazar
<writer>	Jana Goebel
<digital artist>	Martin Loo
<producer>	Richard McCabe
<programmer>	Valerie Ng
<hardware>	Apple Macintosh
<software>	Macromedia Flash
</frameset>	
<noframes>	

	

</pageref>
<220><lhp>

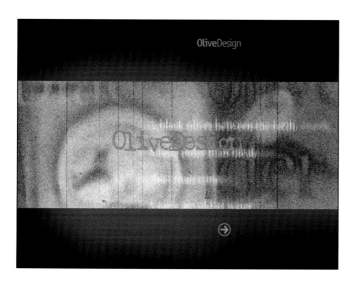

<html>
<head>

<category>	Self-Promotion-CD-ROM</head>
<award>	Merit</title>
<agency>	OliveDesign/Austin
<client>	OliveDesign
<art director>	Kenan Aktulun
<writer>	Todd Alley
<digital artists>	Kenan Aktulun Chad Huff
<photographer>	Kyla Kanz
<producer>	Kyla Kanz
<multimedia>	OliveDesign
<programmer>	Chad Huff
<creative director>	Kenan Aktulun
<hardware>	Apple Macintosh
<software>	Adobe AfterEffects, Adobe Illustrator, Adobe Photoshop Macromedia Director, MediaCleanerPro, Quicktime

</frameset>
<noframes>

</pageref>
<221><rhp>

\<html>
\<head>

\<category>	Self-Promotion-CD-ROM\</head>
\<award>	Merit\</title>
\<agency>	tinderbox interactive/Cape Town
\<client>	tinderbox interactive
\<art directors>	George Galanakis Clint Bryce
\<writers>	Sarah Powys, Jacqui L'Ange Christopher Charles
\<digital artists>	Jamie Meyer, George Galanakis, Francois van Reenan
\<producer>	Christopher Charles
\<multimedia>	tinderbox interactive
\<programmers>	Marcus van Malsen, Paul Messiter-Tooze
\<creative directors>	Jacqui L'Ange, Clint Bryce
\<hardware>	Apple Macintosh, PC
\<software>	Adobe AfterEffects, Adobe Photoshop, Adobe Premier Macromedia Director, Macromedia Flash, Macromedia FreeHand, Macromedia SoundEdit 16, Smacker

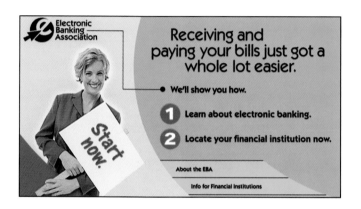

\<html\>
\<head\>

\<category\>	Non Profit Organizations-Web Sites\</head\>
\<award\>	Merit\</title\>
\<agency\>	Euro RSCG DSW Partners/Salt Lake City
\<client\>	The Electronic Banking Association
\<url\>	www.e-banking.org
\<art directors\>	Kim Bellomy
	Tom James
\<writer\>	Chadwick Greenhalgh
\<photographer\>	Michael Schoenfeld
\<producers\>	Ron Hendricks
	Tamy Salem
\<programmers\>	Rob Stringham
	Larry Nybo
\<creative directors\>	Chadwick Greenhalgh
	Kim Bellomy
\<hardware\>	PC
\<software\>	Adobe Photoshop
	Adobe Illustrator
	Uleaded Gif Animator

\</frameset\>
\<noframes\>
\<br\>\<br\>

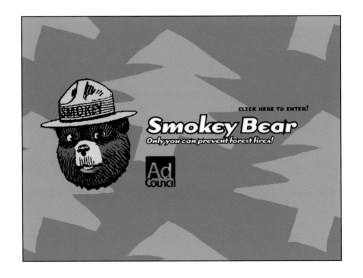

\<html\>
\<head\>

\<category\>	Non Profit Organizations-Web Sites\</head\>
\<award\>	Merit\</title\>
\<agency\>	R/GA Interactive/New York
\<client\>	Ad Council
\<url\>	www.smokeybear.com
\<art director\>	Vincent Lacava
\<writer\>	Alison Blank
\<digital artists\>	Winston Thomas Esther Baek
\<producer\>	Eleanor Tsang
\<programmers\>	Scott Prindle Ephraim Cohen Greg Glass
\<creative director\>	Frank Lantz
\<hardware\>	Apache
\<software\>	CGI, HTML, JAVA, JavaScript Macromedia Shockwave

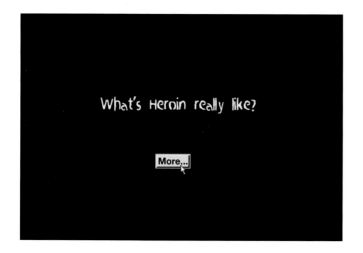

<html>
<head>

<category>	Non Profit Organizations-Other Digital Advertising</head>
<award>	Merit</title>
<agency>	Leo Burnett/Singapore
<client>	National Council Against Drug Abuse
<art director>	Ding Yew Moong
<writer>	Graham Kelly
<digital artist>	Valerie Ng
<producer>	Richard McCabe
<multimedia>	Human Interaction Technologies (HIT)
<programmer>	Valerie Ng
<creative director>	Graham Kelly
<hardware>	PC
<software>	Adobe Illustrator Adobe Photoshop Macromedia Director

</frameset>
<noframes>

</pageref>
<225><rhp>

<html>
<head>

<category>	Non Profit Organizations-Other Digital Advertising</head>
<award>	Merit</title>
<agency>	Leo Burnett/Singapore
<client>	National Council Against Drug Abuse
<art director>	Ding Yew Moong
<writer>	Graham Kelly
<digital artist>	Valerie Ng
<producer>	Richard McCabe
<multimedia>	Human Interaction Technologies (HIT)
<programmer>	Valerie Ng
<creative director>	Graham Kelly
<hardware>	PC
<software>	Adobe Illustrator
	Adobe Photoshop
	Macromedia Director

</frameset>
<noframes>

</pageref>
<226><lhp>

ABSOLUT BEAST.

Absolut Vodka
Add compaign
Click to enlarge

Photography

festival
at Carnegie Hall

Concept for 1998 NY
Jazz Festival poster
Click to enlarge

Abstract Self Portrait
Click to enlarge

<html>
<head>

<category>	College Competition-Other Digital Advertising</head>
<award>	Merit</title>>
<college>	School of Visual Arts/New York
<art director>	Alex Belomlinsky
<writer>	Paul Katz
<digital artist>	Alex Belomlinsky
<producer>	Alex Belomlinsky
<programmer>	Alex Belomlinsky
<hardware>	PC
<software>	3D Studio Max2
	Adobe Illustrator
	Adobe Photoshop
	Adobe Premier
	Macromedia Director
	Macromedia Dreamweaver
	Macromedia Flash

</frameset>
<noframes>

</pageref>
<227><rhp>

<index>
<corporate profiles>

<agency> Bozell Worldwide • Detroit

<address> 1000 Town Center, Suite 1500
Southfield, MI 48075

<telephone> (248) 354-5400

<fax> (248) 358-2422

<home pages> www.bozell.com
www.bozellworldwide.com
www.webspot.com

<key personnel>

<president> Michael J. Vogel

<chief creative officer> Gary Topolewski

<executive creative
director> Bill Morden

<creative director> Sam Ajluni

<interactive associate
creative directors> Peter Arndt, John Gregory

<interactive account
executive> Rod Rakic

<details>

<year founded> 1921

<employees> 700 (Detroit and Field Offices)

<clients> DaimlerChrysler Corporation
Consumer Energy
FSI Council of North America
Federal-Mogul
Little Caesar Enterprises
Meritor Automotive
Shopvac Corporation
Valassis Communications

<overview> Bozell is a full-service global advertising agency focused on each client's business and committed to delivering quality-driven creative solutions to meet and exceed client's marketing challenges.

<design philosophy> On the Web, "Close to the Customer" can be measured in clicks. To keep the clicks up we keep the file sizes down, the creative unexpected and the execution highly interactive.

Bozell – We Build Brands

<services> Believing in the importance of strategic alignment and creative consistency in building brand images, Bozell offers clients a full range of marketing services, including broadcast, print interactive media, direct mail and support materials.

<values> Integrity. Innovation. Trust.

Bozell's values include an ever-present conviction whereby ethics, honesty and respect for every individual guide our actions. We are dedicated to forward thinking and creativity, and hold an uncompromising belief, which enables us to maintain strong "Close to the Customer" client and consumer ties, as well as internal relationships.

</frameset>
<noframes>

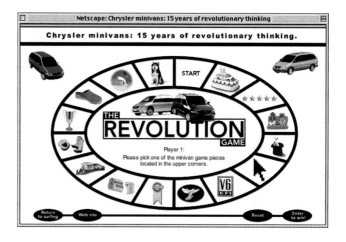

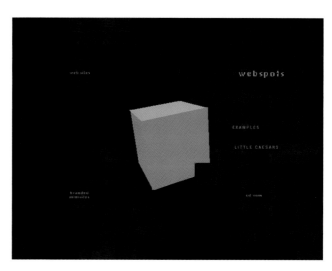

</pageref>
229 <rhp>

<head>
<Agency>
</pic>

COHN & WELLS PARTNERS
EURO RSCG

<agency>	Cohn & Wells Partners EURO RSCG	**<details>**	
<address>	909 Montgomery Street, Suite 300	<year founded>	1984
	San Francisco, CA 94133	<employees>	160
<telephone>	(415) 705-6600	<interactive clients served>	Aristotole.org
<fax>	(415) 705-6624		Bell Canada
<email>	info@cohnwellspartners.com		Blue Shield of California
<home page>	www.cohnwellspartners.com		CarClub.com
<locations>	San Francisco, New York, Los Angeles,		Carrier
	Toronto, Melbourne, and Sydney		Cisco Systems

<key personnel>

<managing partners>	John Greer
	Michael Kantrow
	Susan Murphy
<partners>	Brad Benton, Richard Bernstein,
	Dianne Cullen, Christine Gardner,
	Kevin McCarthy, Mike McGovern,
	Paul Trantanella

interactive clients served (cont.):
Comedy Central
eVoice
First USA
Hennessy
MCI
MyLifepath.com
Sony
Swatch
Telstra
USA.NET
Wells Fargo
Worldlyinvestor.com

<mission> | Provide our clients with the most creative, innovative, measurable and effective ideas...EVER...based on a singular belief that building brands and building sales are one and the same.

<overview> | Cohn & Wells Partners EURO RSCG is redefining what integrated communications means for the digital age. We combine the results orientation and analytical perspective of a premier direct marketing agency with the branding expertise you would expect from a general agency. These skills, combined with world-class technology and extensive experience with interactive marketers, enable us to deliver highly effective, seamlessly integrated communications across all traditional and new media.

<services> | We handle all facets of campaign development and execution, from up front planning to post analysis. Additionally, we are one of the few agencies in the country with a full-service, in-house database management division—so we are well-positioned to build and maintain marketing databases and provide sophisticated data analysis, including predictive modeling.

<interactive unit> | Our full-service interactive unit has quickly become one of the fastest growing areas of our business. Leveraging our brand building expertise, direct marketing perspective and database management capabilities, we handle all facets of interactive advertising programs, including strategy, creative development, production, programming, media planning and buying, analysis and database integration. Our work includes e-mail programs, banner advertising campaigns, e-commerce Web site development and Web-based applications.

</frameset>
</pageref> <noframes>
230 <lhp>

\<agency> **C3 Incorporated**

\<address> 419 Park Avenue South, 5th Floor
New York, New York 10016

\<telephone> (212) 252-2550

\<fax> (212) 252-1180

\<home page> www.c3inc.com

\<details>

\<year founded> 1989

\<clients> Leading international companies in high technolology, financial services, publishing, and arts/entertainment as well as prominent public and private organizations.

\<overview> Image management for brand building is our primary focus. As a result, C3 was one of the first firms to emphasize the strategic role that the Web could play in brand support.

Because we've always viewed the Internet within the framework of the entire communications mix, we work to create electronic presences that reinforce and extend the whole.

\<philosophy> We believe that design is a way of thinking...of expressing solutions in tangible form. Our creative skills are tools that can be applied across varied disciplines to analyze and resolve business challenges. This forms the basis for our product and service conceptual development, and it has led us to develop unique management processes and methods.

\<point of difference> Our approach bridges identity, graphic design and marketing communications to create cohesive, brand-enhancing programs with proven advantages greater than those of "integrated" efforts. (Plus, it keeps things interesting.)

\<mission> Always to deliver simple, effective, engaging solutions,

\<values> To build lasting relationships with our clients based on mutual respect and trust,

To create a workplace where accomplishment is valued, recognized and rewarded,

\<services> The three "Cs" stand for consulting, communications and concepts for products and services. We work across the spectrum from planning through implementation.

\<recognition> We appreciate the hundreds of awards we've received from prestigious competitions and publications such as this one.

\</frameset>
\<noframes>
\
\

<company> DM9DDB

<address> Av. Dr. Cardoso de Mello, 1155
Zip code: 04548-004
São Paulo – SPBrazil

<telephone> (5511) 3040-4999

<fax> (5511) 820-1971

<email> pjpereira@dm9ddb.com.br

<home page> www.dm9.com.br

<key personnel>

<chief executive officer
creative director> Nizan Guanaes

<interactive media
creative director> Paulo Jorge Pereira

<**overview**> "Creation" of online actions that are
independent or integrated into the clients'
offline campaigns, always with a creative
approach and focus on results.

<**mission**> Bring significant results with creative
interactive media work.

<**services**> - Branding and e-commerce planning
and consultancy.
- online media planning and buying.
- Information architecture and
interactive design.
- System integration.

<**recognition**> Cannes Festival – Cyber Lions
International Advertising Creative Week -
1998

One Show – Merit Award
Johnson & Johnson - 1999

Art Directors Club – Merit Award
Post Office – 1999

Cannes Festival – Cyber Lions
UOL (Universo Online) – 1999

Advertising Age International
Cyberstar - 1999

</frameset>
<noframes>

<**details**>

<year founded> DM9DDB's interactive division was
established in March 1997.

<clients> Among the clients DM9DDB's interactive
division has been working for are:
Microsoft, Compaq, Johnson & Johnson,
UOL (Universo Online), Itaú Bank, Itaú
Insurance, Honda and Antarctica beer.

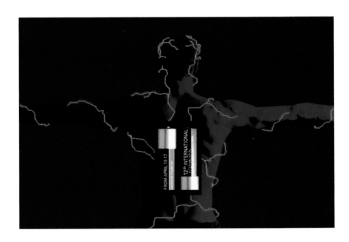

</pageref>
232><lhp>

E.ON INTERACTIVE DESIGN   </pic>

<agency> E.ON Interactive

<address> 412 Cedar Street
Suite E
Santa Cruz, CA 95060

<telephone> (831) 420-2660

<fax> (831) 471-9852

<email> adam@eoninteractive.com

<homepage> www.eoninteractive.com

<key personnel>

<chief executive officer> Adam Fleischer

<vice president> Vince Doherty

<details>

<year founded> 1993

<employees> 15

<clients> 3Com
Lucent
Sun Microsystems
Cisco Systems
Hewlett-Packard
Acer

<overview> E.ON Interactive is a full-service multimedia agency based near Silicon Valley. Since 1993, we've been a leader in the design and development of high-level Web and CD-ROM based interactive communications projects for sales, marketing, training, and education.

We create strategic-minded interactive communications that creatively convey our clients' messages via the effective use of today's evolving interactive and multimedia technology solutions.

Our hands-on experience in the corporate and high-tech worlds enables us to understand your company and your audience. E.ON will energize your marketing, sales and training projects. E.ON will help build your image and deliver bottom-line results.

E.ON will guide you through the fast-changing world of interactive communications so that you can focus on business. Our experienced team can handle every aspect of your project – from identifying your critical communications needs to complex programming.

<recognition> We have received considerable recognition for the work we've produced. Our awards include the One Club Merit Award, an MC ICON award sponsored by Business Week for "The Best in High Technology Marketing Communications," a Business Marketing Association ProComm award, plus the Addy award, the CINDY, and a Gold Hugo.

</frameset>
<noframes>

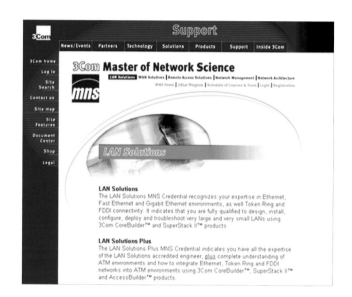

</pageref>
<233><rhp>

<head>
<Agency>

</pic>

<agency> EURO RSCG DSW Partners

<address> 4 Triad Center #400
Salt Lake City, UT 84180

<telephone> (801) 364-0919

<fax> (801) 536-7350

<home page> www.dsw.com

<key personnel>

<partner> John Dahlin

<partner/executive creative director> Kim Carter

<senior vp account director> Peter Klinge

<overview> DSW Partners is an integrated online and offline branding agency, producing award-winning interactive, print, and broadcast communications. We work with some of the premier companies in the technology industry. And, because we're based in Salt Lake City, we get a great lifestyle and environment to boot.

<mission> We build killer brands that make people comfortable with technology.

<services> Want a SuperBowl TV Spot? We'll shoot it. Want a print campaign? We'll do it. And then we'll create the Website and online ad campaign to support it, too. The result? Our clients get consistent, integrated branding campaigns from start to finish. All while working with just one agency. And since we're part of the EURO RSCG network, our communications are truly global.

Our online staff is constantly pushing the bounds of technology, creating award-winning work that grabs and retains customers. We pride ourselves on brilliant strategic thinking, flawless execution, and innovative quality-assurance and research, including eye-tracking.

<ancient history> We launched Intel Inside. We were Netscape's first interactive shop. We created the Iomega brand and helped Zip drives take off. We even produced the first interactive SuperBowl TV commercial.

<recognition> DSW Partners was recently ranked by Ad Age as the eighth most award-winning interactive agency in the world. And you've seen our work in this book. That about says it all.

<details>

<year founded> 1986

<employees> 200+

<clients> Ask Jeeves
CheckFree
InFocus
Intel
Iomega
Minolta PPD
PointServe
Red Lobster
Sequent
Sportsnuts.com
Storagetek
Telocity
Tenfold
Xircom

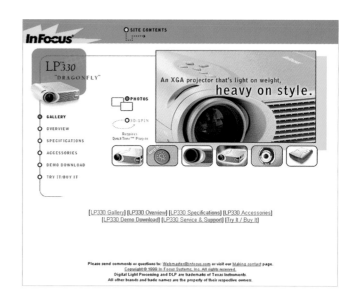

</pageref>
<234><lhp>

<want a job?> We're continually looking for talented, driven people who love the Web. We need art directors, writers, multimedia designers, account supervisors, technologists, producers, and pretty much anyone else who wants to produce outstanding work for real clients in a great work and play environment. Send your samples, URL and/or resume to webjobs@dsw.com.

</frameset>
<noframes>

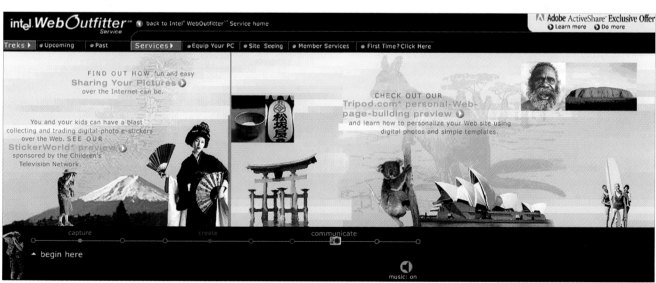

</pageref>
<235><rhp>

<head>
<Agency>

</pic>

<agency>   Genex

<address>   10003 Washington Blvd.
Los Angeles, CA 90232

<telephone>   (310) 736-2000

<fax>   (310) 736-2001

<email>   info@genex.com

<home page>   www.genex.com

key personnel

<ceo/
engineering director>   Walter Schild

<creative director>   David Glaze

<marketing director>   Dalin Clark

<details>

<year founded>   1995

<employees>   65

<select clients>   American Honda/Acura
e-Insurance Systems
Herman Miller Inc.
IZ.com
Nestlé USA
The Patent and License Exchange
Porsche Cars North America
State Street Corporation
Sterling Commerce
Sterling Software
The Warner Bros. Network
SFNB Bank

<overview>   Genex is a tightly integrated group of smart, creative professionals with a shared passion for building innovative digital business solutions. We have diverse backgrounds in advertising, technology, consulting and entertainment, and bring the benefits of these combined experiences to our clients. Now in our fifth year of business, Genex remains one of the largest independent interactive firms in the US.

As the interactive industry continues its rapid growth, Genex has seen client requirements change dramatically and we've evolved our business accordingly. In many cases, we're hired for our special ability to effectively combine business strategy, engineering and creative. We are staunch believers in the value of branding and have helped many clients develop and extend their brands online with measurable results.

<genex strategy>   We take time to understand the key points of success and failure within a client's business model and then address those issues with specific interactive applications, many of them unique to Genex. Our Strategy Group focuses on helping clients make informed decisions that will strengthen their corporate position in the competitive online environment.

The insight of the Genex Strategy Group is a strength that benefits all our clients. As Interactive Agency of Record for many, we take seriously the role of trusted advisor as well as developer. Members of our Engineering Group also act as consultants, and are highly skilled at interfacing with clients' in-house technical staff to create robust, scalable and solid technical components with future development in mind.

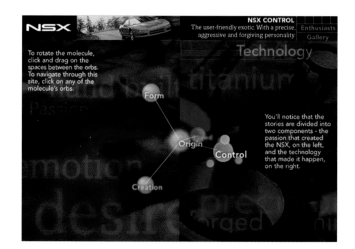

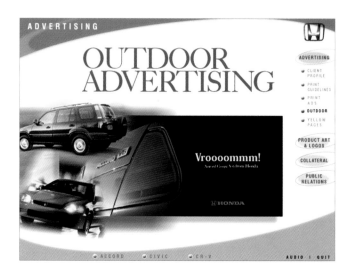

</pageref>
<236><thp>

Genex is committed to project management, and we've created a unique development process that structures every job for a successful solution. Most of our competitors say the same thing, but we really believe our methodology is something special.

We naturally start each project with a careful evaluation of its business implications, marketing goals and audience demographics. This creates a foundation for the development of all strategic, creative and technical plans, and ensures our solutions are industry-competitive, on target, and functional for both the audience and the client. Then the workflow is discussed and documented. Several phases, including creative and technical design and user interface and copy development, execute in tandem for efficiency. And a password-protected, customized Project Site is created on our

development server, giving clients and group members around-the-clock access to weekly updates, status reports, work in progress and a site map. It looks simple enough on paper. The trick is in the execution.

Together, the Genex groups offer a thorough understanding of front-end marketing and branding strategies tied to sophisticated back-end implementations. Genex advancements in site personalization, e-commerce, database development, and custom applications have typically resulted in happy clients, expanded relationships and multiple referrals. We must be doing something right.

```
</frameset>
<noframes>
<br><br>
```

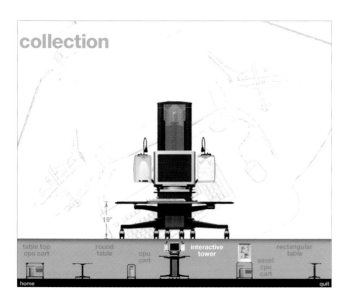

```
</pageref>
237><rhp>
<br><br>
```

interactive8, inc. \</pic\>

\<**agency**\> interactive8, inc.

\<address\> 114 West 26th Street
12th Floor
New York, NY 10001

\<locations\> New York and San Francisco

\<telephone\> (212) 807-1762

\<fax\> (212) 807-1763

\<email\> info@interactive8.com

\<home page\> www.interactive8.com

\<**key personnel**\>

\<president\> Douglas Rice

\<managing partner\> Bill Markel

\<new business\> Doug Sundheim, Lary Tuckett,
Declan Rennick

\<creative director\> Howard Coale, David Lewis

\<associate media director\> Chris Neuner

\<services\> Creative Development-Web Site, Banner
Strategic Planning and Consulting
Ethnic Marketing
online and Off-line Promotions/Publicity
Media Planning & Buying
Hosting, Tracking and Analysis
E-Commerce
Technology-Custom Programming,
Integration & Database Development

\<**creating a web presence
that delivers**\> Interactive8 is one of New York's
most prominent full-service interactive
advertising agencies. From the beginning
we were ingrained with the notion of
doing something different: serving the
brand, not the agency. The agency sets
itself apart from the competition by
adding two key elements to the mix:
long-range strategic planning and high-end
client service.

From our initial strategic vision to our
client's long term business goals, we use
our client's marketing message as the focal
point for all of our strategic, creative and
technical development.

As a result, our online projects do more
than just engage and entertain people,
they deliver specific, targeted results
for the clients we serve. A&E Television
Networks, M&M/Mars and Maybelline are
just a few of the world's most prestigious
companies that have benefited from
Interactive8's methods and expertise
in leveraging their brands online and
integrating online and offline branding
programs. We have developed an expertise
in bringing communications/media
and packaged goods companies online,
with a specialty in marketing to young
adult consumers.

\<**details**\>

\<year founded\> 1994

\<employees\> 100

\<clients\> A&E Television Networks
AT&T
DeBeers
Human Rights Watch
ibeauty
Investors in People U.K.
Maybelline
M&M/Mars
PhoneFree.com
World Wrestling Federation

\<**finding unusual
solutions**\> We devise sites that push the online
experience beyond convention by
implementing applications in unusual
ways. The Design Your Own Engagement
Ring application allows consumers for
the first time to create personalized
engagement rings online, then print

out the design and take it to their local jeweler to have it made. Alternatively, the award-winning "M&M's" Network™is based on a online network model, similar to television, built on multiple self-contained yet interconnected content channels, each targeted at a different segment of the brand's audience. The site gives users access to seven different online channels of branded entertainment content, each of which appeals to a different audience of "M&M's"® lovers.

‹creating communities› The HistoryChannel.com is regarded as the premier history portal on the Web. It brings together history buffs and educators, uniting users with similar interests in one destination. Another community site, Maybelline.com creates an online community by combining message boards, polls and an online contest searching for five young women to represent Maybelline for the coming year.

‹expanded marketing opportunities› Interactive8's three core disciplines of strategy, creative and technology are supported by our multiple divisions that specialize in online media planning and buying, offline promotions/publicity and ethnic marketing. We have found spectacular return on investment results from supporting the initial strategy and site development with a variety of creative promotional efforts.

‹relationships› Our strong relationships with clients are built over time. As we learn the details of a client's business, we apply our extensive knowledge of new media to their unique strengths and needs. Then we develop proactive strategies, constantly encouraging our clients to push their marketing potential beyond current boundaries.

Our clients depend upon us to stay ahead of the curve in technology and Internet marketing... and our results show just that.

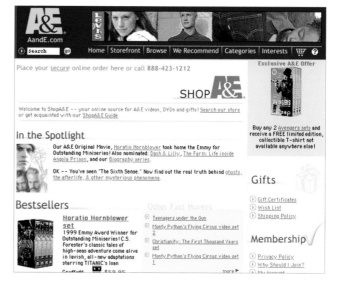

<agency> Internet Solutions Partners

<address> 75 Maiden Lane, 4th Floor
New York, NY 10038

<telephone> (212) 402-6804

<fax> (212) 402-6809

<email> rene@isppartners.com

<home page> www.isppartners.com

<key personnel>

<ceo> Rene Jimenez

<cio> Armando Roman

<senior design director> Yenni Zhang

<vp of sales/business development> Darren Sager

<director of client services> Monique Rubio

<overview> Internet Solutions Partners (ISPPartners) is a full-service new media design, systems integration and database marketing firm based in New York City. We specialize in driving traffic to Web site, Web design/development and integration of Internet applications for leading global brands. By bringing together dynamic content, interactivity and elegant, logical design we create Web sites that establish loyal followings and generate real returns for our clients and strategic partners. Our staff has real world corporate experience working with some of the largest E-commerce companies in the world.

<mission> ISPPartners' mission is simple: we create beautifully designed, highly functional Web sites that inform, engage and empower our client's customers. We then design and produce a Web site marketing strategy that works for you. And because each client has different needs and objectives, all of our work is customized to order. Every project is custom designed to satisfy the precise needs of the target client base.

We're strong on business basics, like delivering on time and on budget because we ask the right questions up front.

<recognition> ISPPartners has been frequently cited in numerous Internet media sources as well as in design publications such as Industry Standards and Gomez Advisors.com. Independent industry analysts consistently refer to ISPPartners as one of a handful of premier interactive consultancies. Recent recognition includes Media Metrics and Adage which have ranked several of our properties among the top 10 in their respective categories.

<services> ISPPartners covers the full digital spectrum: strategic planning, Web site design and production, media planning and placement, banner design and database marketing. The company has developed a number of innovative Web-based business applications providing a "turnkey" solution for diverse range of clients' electronic commerce needs.

Our specialty is understanding the big picture. Each of our projects results in a customized solution to meet specific objectives. From project planning to creative concept, design and execution, ISPPartners offers complete interactive services. Additional in-house expertise includes online media buying and planning, database programming and integration, navigation and interface design, e-commerce development, hosting,

</pageref>
<240><lhp>

statistical site traffic reporting and database marketing.

We integrate the proper mix of services to help our clients achieve all of their marketing and overall business goals. We begin all our projects with an intensive study of our clients' marketing needs. We ask questions, review data and evaluate past campaigns to ensure that we understand their brand as fully as possible.

<feature works>

www.tradingdirect.com
www.speedyclick.com
www.shochettrading.com
www.bookdigital.com

<our philosophy>

We believe strongly in approaching projects from the perspective of the user and we work to integrate clients' corporate communications strategies across all media to provide consistent branding. Hi priority

is placed on user interface, design and ease of navigation. We believe interactive projects benefit from simplicity in design and copy. It's important to strike a balance with developing technologies to ensure that the message gets top billing, with additional support from the technology. We focus on stability and performance as top technical priorities.

All communications revolving around a brand should be integrated, working together to deliver a consistent tone and image to customers. Current materials and strategies are always reviewed and incorporated to ensure integrity of brand personality.

</frameset>
<noframes>

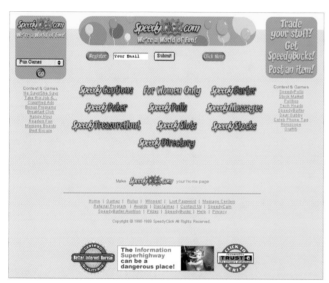

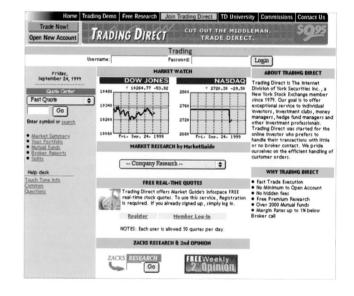

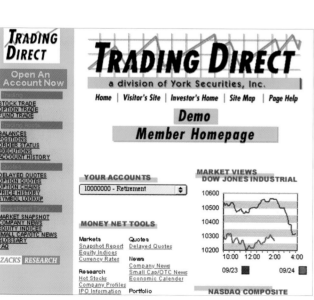

</pageref>
<241><rhp>

interactive advertising

<agency> Lot21 Interactive Advertising Group, Inc.

<address> 548 Fourth Street
San Francisco, CA 94107

<telephone> (415) 227-2121

<fax> (415) 227-2138

<email> info@lot21.com

<home page> www.lot21.com

key personnel

<president/ceo> Kate Everett-Thorp

<coo> Eric Wheeler

<cto> Mark Avnet

<media director> Mark Stephens

<creative director> Paco Vinoly

<director of consulting> Norma Manty

<accounts director> Lyn Rundell

<director.tech design> Sasha Pave

<director of business development> Andrew O'Dell

<details> Details

<year founded> February 1998

<employees> 90

<clients> BankAmerica
Beautyscene
Blue Shield of CA
E-Stamp
iOwn
KBkids
Onsale
Real Media
Respond.com
Seagate
Webvan
Works.com

<overview> Lot21 is an interactive marketing, media, and advertising agency specializing in the creation of integrated marketing solutions for advertisers who want to better target and convert consumers to their brand, products, and services. The team at Lot21 has a comprehensive knowledge of the Internet industry that helps clients exceed their parameters for success providing a true return-on-investment.

<services> Account Services, Media Planning & Buying, Interactive Design (banners, microsite development, rich media, logos), Strategic Consulting.

<mission> The Lot21 team united to accomplish one mission: to contribute to the bottom line of companies wanting to reach consumers online. We do this by designing and executing the most effective online advertising and marketing campaigns—combining strategic planning, creative and media expertise. Our vision entails contributing to effective advertising models as well as shaping the evolution of Interactive advertising.

<design philosophy> Interactive design should perform both technically and aesthetically for the target audience. Palates and techniques are optimized to create rich, striking ads that inform, entertain and, above all, sell or convert customers to your product, brand or service.

Austin Powers browser skin

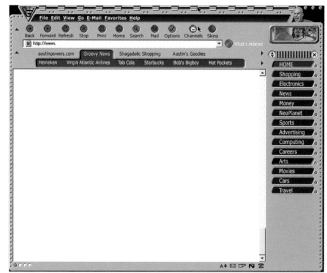

</pageref>
242<lhp>

1999 Cannes Lions international Advertising Festival, Finalist - NationsBank;
April 1999 @d-tech Awards: Gold Award- Onsale atCost Flash Generator Banner, Gold Award - Daewoo Motors, Silver Award - When.com;
March 1999 ClickZ Challenge / Web Advertising '99: Rainmaker Award – Doug Flutie Foundation;
March 1999 One Show Interactive Awards: Pencil Winner - NationsBank Flash Banner Campaign, Finalist - Daewoo Motors;

1998 Advertising Age's Women to Watch awarded to Kate Everett-Thorp, President & CEO of Lot21;
1998 NewMedia Magazine Invision Awards: Gold Award - Environmental Defense Fund, Finalist - NationsBank Flash Banner Campaign.

</frameset>
<noframes>

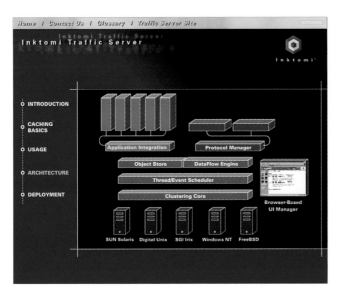

MARTIN INTERACTIVE `</pic>`

`<agency>` Martin Interactive

`<address>` One Shockoe Plaza
Richmond, VA 23219-4132

`<telephone>` (804) 698-8000

`<fax>` (804) 698.8521

`<email>` cmason@mail.martinagency.com

`<home page>` www.martininteractive.com

`<key personnel>`

`<senior vp, managing director>` Claiborne Mason

`<vp, creative director>` Dave Parrish

`<who we are>` The Web has the potential to fundamentally redefine every industry. No business will be untouched by the phenomenal transformation we are witnessing. As a result, we believe that the interactive work we do for our clients should in some way change the way our clients think about their business.

At Martin Interactive, our track record with companies like Coca-Cola is proof of our ability to develop highly successful Web-based marketing programs. And because we are a marketing-oriented interactive agency, we can take your brand – its essence, values, personality and strengths – and effectively translate that into the digital world. We look at your business goals, and make sure your Web strategy is delivering results. These skills, plus our depth of creative and technology talent, make for a unique and extraordinarily effective combination.

`<structure>` Our team is made up of dedicated interactive specialists – strategists, account managers, media planners, writers, art directors, designers and Web developers. These in-house resources allow us to provide turnkey digital services, from site development and Websites advertising to intranets, extranets and other business solutions.

`</frameset>`
`<noframes>`
`<br><br>`

`<details>`

`<year founded>` 1994

`<employees>` 25

`<clients>` The Coca-Cola Company
FMC Agricultural
Gerber
Marriott
- Fairfield Inn
- Residence Inn
- SpringHill Suites
- TownePlace Suites
Novartis Consumer Health
PageNet
Pulsar
Scott & Stringfellow
Seiko
Smart Online
Vertex Pharmaceuticals
Yellow Pages Publishers Association

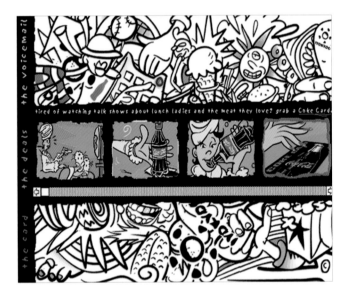

<agency> Nicholson NY

<address> 295 Lafayette Street
The Puck Building
8th Floor
New York, NY 10012

<telephone> (212) 274-0470

<fax> (212) 274-0380

<email> reach_us@nny.com

<homepage> www.nny.com

<key personnel>

<ceo> Tom Nicholson

<evp> Chad Gallant

<partial client list>
American Cancer Society
Chubb Group of Insurance Companies
E*TRADE
General Motors
H&R Block
The Mashantucket Pequot Nation
Medcast Networks
The Metropolitan Museum of Art
New York Daily News
Pfizer
Product News Network (PNN)
Reader's Digest
Sony
Thomas Publishing
Wall Street Rarities
WebMD

<mission> Nicholson NY is singularly focused on partnering with clients to create customer-focused e-business applications that extend online commerce beyond the transaction and into a full relationship experience. We employ a rigorous process that incorporates best-in-class business and strategic consulting, design and technical engineering to understand our client's business, marketing and communications goals and execute interactive solutions to help meet them.

<approach> The Nicholson way is to put strategy first. We begin each assignment by coming to a full understanding of the business, marketing and communications objectives we are trying to meet. From there, we partner with our clients to develop a plan for how interactive technologies can be applied to achieve the objectives. This provides a road map for the design and technology groups. At each stage we concentrate not only on the quality of our solution, but on delivering that solution at the speed of business today.

<expertise> Three core capabilities – strategy, design and technology – allow us to offer end-to-end solutions to our customers. On a tactical level, the services we offer include marketing and business strategy, media planning and buying, graphic design, content creation, information architecture, database management and integration, and custom software development.

<best in class talent> Our strategists, designers, engineers, media buyers and planners are Nicholson's key assets, but their true strength is achieved when they work as a team, bringing their varied backgrounds and expertise to bear on our client's businesses. That's why Advertising Age ranked Nicholson NY #3 internationally in its list of top creative interactive agencies.

</frameset>
<noframes>

</pageref>
245 <rhp>

Ogilvy Interactive
worldwide </pic>

<agency>   OgilvyInteractive South Africa

<head office>   18 Roeland Street, Gardens, Cape Town
<address>   South Africa, 8001

<mailing address>   PO Box 1142, Cape Town, 8000
South Africa

<telephone>   +27 (21) 467-1400

<fax>   +27 (21) 467-1401

<email>   info@oi.co.za

<home pages>   www.oi.co.za

<studios>   Cape Town, Johannesburg and Durban

<key personnel>

<chairman>   David Burstein

<deputy chairman>   Duncan Forrest

<managing director>   Roger Horrocks

<creative director>   Damian Stephens

<executive producer>   Jack Krüger

<overview>   OgilvyInteractive South Africa is the interactive arm of Ogilvy and Mather South Africa, the biggest communications group in South Africa, and part of the Ogilvy Interactive Worldwide Network. Working closely with the specialist groups and disciplines of the overall company offering, OgilvyInteractive South Africa ensures a single brand vision with all marketing and advertising strategies taking full advantage of the emerging digital medium.

<mission>   To be most valued by those who most value brands.

<services>   Within the conceptual matrix of 360° Branding and Customer Ownership Wired, OgilvyInteractive South Africa has evolved a range of interactive offerings designed to help our clients build brands, customer equity and loyalty.

<design philosophy>   Our design is based on a belief in the power of brands and great ideas, and a commitment to help our clients solve real business problems on time and within budget.

<values>   Fresh Ideas. Immaculate Execution. Teamwork. Our objective is to be successful by making our clients successful.

<employment>   As we continue to grow to meet clients' demands, we are constantly on the lookout for great new people to infuse our prodigious culture with talent. Those hungry for the experience of working in an exciting interactive environment on the tip of Africa can send their resumés to joinus@oi.co.za.

<details>

<year founded>   1996

<employees>   22

<clients>   Armscor
Consolidated Bullion
Defy
Gryphon Asset Management
IBM South Africa
Lotus South Africa
Nedbank
Nedcor Investment Bank
Old Mutual
Polo Clothing
South African Breweries
Telkom
Y2K Decision Support Centre

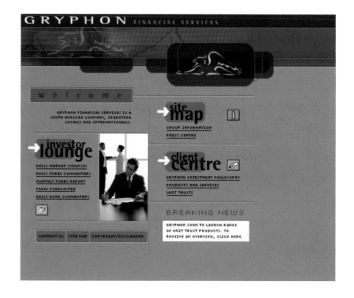

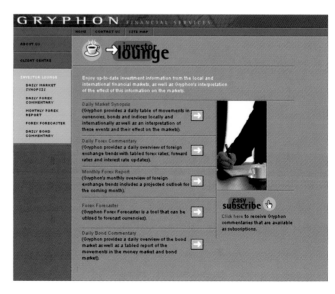

</frameset>
<noframes>

</pageref>
246><lhp>

agency> OgilvyInteractive worldwide

address> 309 West 49th Street
New York, NY 10019-7399

\<telephone\> (212) 237-6000

\<fax\> (212) 237-4138

\<email\> mike.windsor@ogilvy.com

\<home page\> www.ogilvy.com

key personnel>

\<president\> Mike Windsor

\<director,
europe/me/africa\> Philip Greenfield

\<director, north america\> J. Sandom

\<director, asia/pacific\> Todd Chambers

\<director, latin america\> Evandro Paes dos Reis

\<executive creative
director\> Jan Leth

\<interactive media
director\> Susan Schiekofer

details>

\<year founded\> 1984

\<employees\> 400

\<clients\> Arthur Andersen
Ford Motor Company
GTE
IBM
Jaguar
Kimberley Clark
Kodak
Lotus
Nestle
Ortho Biotech
Perrier
SmithKlineBeechum
Streamline
Tivoli
Unilever
WebMD

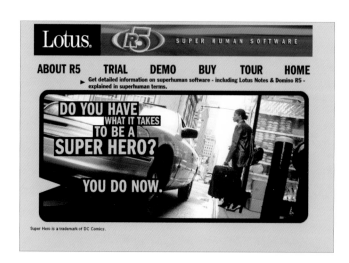

overview> The first global advertising agency with a dedicated interactive capability (beginning in 1984), today, OgilvyInteractive is the largest integrated interactive agency in the world, with 22 offices and 12 service bureaus serving more than 40 countries.

With the full leverage of a global communications agency, we produce one-to-one marketing solutions online that build brands, as well as customer equity and loyalty.

We believe that each time a company presents itself on the Web, it is a brand building opportunity, whether it is on a Web site, in an advertising unit, or through a sponsorship. So, we've fully integrated the disciplines of traditional advertising and direct response with cutting-edge interactive technologies to ensure our clients take full advantage of every such opportunity.

values> Candor, curiosity, originality, intellectual rigor, perseverance, brains, and civility.

mission> To grow our client's customer equity in value, volume, and good will.

design philosophy> "It is the professional duty of the advertising agent to conceal his artifice. When Aeschines spoke, they said, 'How well he speaks.' But when Demosthenes spoke, they said, 'Let us march against Philip.' I'm for Demosthenes."

–David Ogilvy, *Confessions of an Advertising Man*

When David Ogilvy first shared this insight, the terms multimedia and interactive had entirely different connotations than they do today. He was, of course, referring to advertising and graphic design for what we now call traditional media – print, broadcast and outdoor. His insight, however, rings as true today as it did 36 years ago. "A good advertisement," Ogilvy said, "is one which sells the product without drawing attention to itself." Likewise, good interactive design inspires its audience to act, or interact, in a manner that is both fluid and intuitive – without drawing attention to itself. To design such an interface, in fact, is the essence of new media artistry.

recognition

• Ranked #1 New Media Agency (first-ever international ranking of creative award winners listed by Advertising Age International, 1999)

• Named one of the Best Top Ten Interactive Agencies by Adweek IQ (1999)

• Named one of the Top Five Leading Agencies by The Red Herring (1998 & 1999)

• Winner of the 1999 Grand Clio, the first ever Interactive award at The Clio Awards (the most prestigious in the international advertising and business communities), as well as a Gold Clio for the IBM e-culture campaign, and a Silver Clio for our work on Tivoli

• Winner of two 1998 CyberLions (first ever award for Interactive at the Cannes Advertising Festival) for IBM Olympics Luge Game (NY) and www.campaign.com (London)

• Awarded another 3 CyberLions in 1999, including the CyberLion Grand Prix, for the online IBM e-culture campaign in both the Rich Media and Beyond the Banner categories

• Three One Show Interactive Pencil awards (1999):

• Gold — IBM e-culture (interactive banner ad campaign)

• Silver — IBM e-culture "PGA" (single interactive banner ad)

• Bronze — IBM e-culture (integrated branding campaign)

• Recipient of a 1999 Andy Award

• Two 1999 Art Directors Club awards

• 1999 MC Icon Award

• 1999 AdTech Award

• 1999 Adweek IQ Marketing Awards (not entered by creative) Best Online and Offline Integrated Campaign

• 1999 Echo Awards finalist

QUANTUM LEAP

agency — Quantum Leap Communications

address — 420 West Huron Street
Chicago, IL 60610

telephone — (312) 595-0400

fax — (312) 595-0012

email — contact@leapnet.com

home page — www.quantum.leapnet.com

key personnel

managing director — Debra Bean

Chief Creative Officer — Richard Giuliani

executive creative director — David Hernandez

director of technology — Matthew Hanson

director of operations — Kris Konno

overview — Quantum Leap is a unique technology and marketing hybrid that partners with Internet-focused companies to build sophisticated e-business solutions and to develop relationship-building marketing campaigns.

From e-commerce, design, and development, to business strategy, advertising and marketing, Quantum Leap champions the needs of the consumer to create engaging online experiences that generate measurable results.

Quantum Leap has been featured in numerous award shows and industry sources including One Show Interactive, @d:tech, ID Magazine, ChannelSeven, ZDTV, PC Magazine, Wall Street Journal Interactive Edition and CIO Magazine.

details

year founded — 1994

employees — 90

clients — American Airlines
Anheuser-Busch
Capitol Records
Ernst & Young
FTD
Microsoft Encarta
Microsoft Slate
Morningstar
MSNBC
MSN Internet Access
Nike
Sam's Club
Sportsline USA, Inc.
The Tribune Corporation
The University of Chicago Graduate School of Business
Wal-Mart

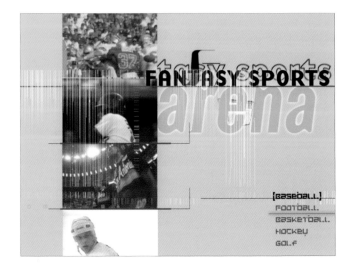

<Featured Work>

American Airlines
aa.com site redesign

Microsoft Encarta
Rich media campaign featuring Quick Time
VR jump page

Nike
Niketown multimedia presentation system

Tribune Corporation
Metromix arts & entertainment guide

CBS Sportsline
Multimedia presentation system

Ernst & Young
Profile-driven extranet

<Opportunities at
Quantum Leap>

Join a company that develops compelling interactive solutions for some of the world's best-known brands. Quantum Leap has employment opportunities across all disciplines including business strategy, design, information architecture, account management, production and technology. E-mail your cover letter and resume to jobs@leapnet.com.

</frameset>
<noframes>

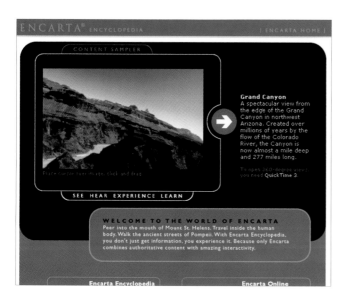

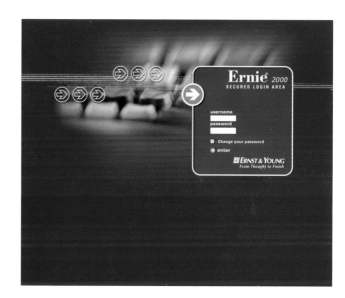

<head>
<Agency>

</pic>

rare MEDIUM INC

<agency> Rare Medium Inc.

<head office address> 2207 Commerce Street
Dallas, TX 75201

<telephone> (214) 742-RARE (7273)

<fax> (214) 742-7274

<homepage> www.raremedium.com

key personnel

<chairman and ceo> Glenn S. Meyers

<president and chief
operating officer> Suresh V. Mathews

<chief technology officer> David Rosenbloom

<chief creative officer> Gong Szeto

overview Rare Medium Group Inc.'s strategy is to
incubate paradigm-shifting ideas and
build the next wave of blockbuster
Internet companies by leveraging its
award winning Internet solutions arm,
Rare Medium Inc., its capital and its
vast network of online relationships.
We have broadened our initial Internet
solutions-based strategy to include a
ventures/incubator business offering
access to capital.

Our success stories include long term
relationships with some of the most
sophisticated brands in the world. Our
clients will tell you, every Rare creation
embodies the talent and experience of our
unique company.

services Rare Medium develops e-commerce
Internet strategies, improves business
processes and develops marketing
communications, branding, strategies,
and interactive content using
Internet-based technologies and solutions.

At Rare Medium, understanding our
clients' business and marketing objectives
is fundamental to our success as a
full-service, interactive solutions agency.
By looking beyond the scope of a project,
we strive to develop strategies designed
to exceed and redefine both long and
short-term objectives. Our innovative use
of interactive technology provides our
clients with high level results.

details

<year founded> 1995

<employees> 400

<clients> General Mills
Betty Crocker
Quaker State
Mattel
Neiman Marcus
Microsoft
JP Morgan
Merril Lynch
Bugle Boy
DirectWeb
How to Guru Online
Prodigy Internet
The New York Times
Yahoo! Internet Life
20th Century Fox
Macromedia
Muze
Microsoft
Intel
Compaq
Volvo
Pontiac

<featured work> Intel's Mediadome (sm) -
Re-design, re-launch, and maintenance of
an entertainment and technology Web site.

Neiman Marcus -
The online version of Neiman Marcus'
famed monthly publication "the book."

Fox Interactive -
Re-design, re-launch, and maintenance
of the marketing Website for Fox's
gaming products.

Fox Interactive -
James Cameron's Titanic Explorer CD-ROM
This 3 CD product will be the definitive
Titanic reference for fans and enthusiasts.

Circumstance -
In early 1999, Circumstance was acquired
by Rare Medium. The site attempts to
redefine the boundaries of technology.

Intel's ArtMuseum.net -
This site showcases art exhibitions,
making art more accessible through
Web technologies.

</frameset>
<noframes>

</pageref>
<252><lhp>

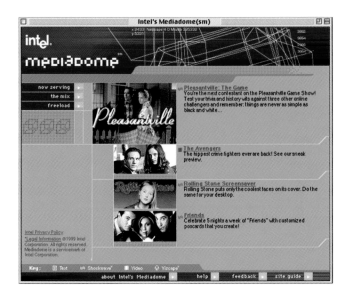

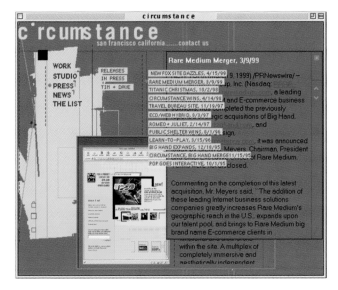

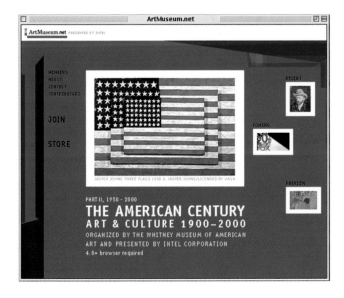

USWeb/CKS </pic>

<agency> USWeb/CKS

<address> 410 Townsend Street
San Francisco, CA 94107

<telephone> 415-369-6700

<homepage> www.uswebcks.com

<key personnel>

<chairman of the board> Mark Kvamme

<ceo> Robert Shaw

<president and coo> Tom Steiner

<chief financial officer> Carolyn Aver

<chief strategist and
knowledge officer> Ian Small

<chief creative officer> Tom Suiter

<**culture**> Right Brain + Left Brain

<**mission**> We are transform businesses for the
digital economy

<**creative soul**> Resist the Usual

<**work**> E-Commmerce, Branding, Advertising,
Network Solutions, Information
Architecture, Knowledge Management,
Environmental Design, Film & Video
Production, Packaging, (breathe here...)
Change Management, Corporate Strategy,
Customer Relationship Management, and
lots of Top Secret Innovations

<**past lives**> Apple, Novell, Oracle, Weiden & Kennedy,
Ernst & Young, Anderson Consulting,
Silicon Graphics, Landor Associates,
Chiat/Day, MCI, IBM, and many many many
other breeding grounds for next generation
Change Agents

</frameset>
<noframes>

<**details**>

<headquarters> San Francisco

<born> November 1998

<worldwide offices> 50 offices in 22 states and ten countries

<number of
languages spoken> 18

<professionals> 3,800

<total experience in
internet years> 39,549 years

<nasdaq symbol> USWB

<annualized revenues> $330M

<number of acquisitions> 41

<average number of emails
each day> 48,958

<number of
network nodes> 2614 worldwide

<number of fortune
100 clients> 46

</pageref>
<254><thp>

When we look at a statue **OF SOMEONE GREAT,** we think they've got something we don't. We are trained to think that only a tiny percentage of us have the stuff it takes to be a hero. Not many of us will cure any diseases or slay any dragons, but every single one of us, **EVERY SINGLE ONE OF US,** is called to be a king, a queen, a hero in our ordinary lives. We don't build statues to worship the exceptional life, we build them **to remind ourselves what is POSSIBLE IN OUR OWN.**

‹ MORE ›

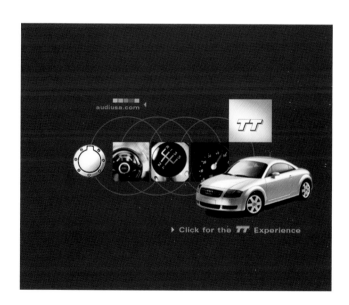

<head>
<Agency> </pic>

<agency>	Webfactory Ltd.
<address>	9 Baggot Court Lower Baggot Street Dublin 2 Ireland
<telephone>	+353 (1)-678-9992
<fax>	+353 (1)-662-5970
<email>	info@webfactory.ie
<homepage>	www.webfactory.ie

<key personnel>

<managing director>	John O'Shea
<technical director>	Simon Walsh
<development director>	Ronan MacRuairi
<creative director>	Marcus Lynam

<overview>

We're not the usual run-of-the-mill Internet agency. Really, we're not.

We have the silverware; Irish Web Design Agency of the Year in 1998, national advertising accolades from ICAD, and international recognition from One Show Interactive, EPICA, UK Design Week and the European Design Annual.

We have the skills; consultancy, design, programming, copywriting, eCommerce, hosting, PR, online media buying and advertising services.

We have the clients; Ireland's largest mobile phone operator, the country's main electricity and gas companies, three of Ireland's top seven insurance companies as well as sites for clients in the entertainment, consumer, fitness, real estate, financial and aviation industries. (Our client base also continues to grow in the UK and Europe.)

We have the experience; major projects include broker extranets, banking solutions, online retailing, Shockwave/Flash games and extensive legacy system integration.

The difference is in our attitude - the way we approach each project, each problem and each delivered solution. We believe that you don't have to be serious, to be serious about what you do, and we think it shows. Our clients can vouch they've got Websites that do exactly what they wanted them to do, delivered on time and within budget, but we're still sane, still have lives, and a sense of humour intact.

Talk to our people. Visit our office. Look at our sites. Send us your résumé. You'll notice the difference too.

<www.oceanfree.net> oceanfree.net is the first ISP in Ireland to offer free Internet access and email to business and residential users. Webfactory was involved in many aspects of the site's development, including writing the software that provisioned the users' email accounts.

<www.thecommonwealth.org> The Commonwealth Secretariat carries out the priorities of its 54-member governments. Its Website includes comprehensive information about the Commonwealth, publications and journals, meetings and events and a regularly updated Spotlight section of latest press releases and articles from the organization.

</pageref>
256 <lhp>

<Guardian Insurance Broker Extranet: Keynet>

Guardian PMPA Insurance is Ireland's largest non-life insurer, with over 530,000 policy holders. Webfactory developed Keynet to offer brokers full, secure and real-time access to Guardian's insurance applications, replacing paper processing with online verification. Keynet enables brokers to interact with the Guardian database, delivering full quotations, new business inception, mid-term adjustments, and the printing of insurance certificates, along with access to the brokers' own financial accounts.

<www.eircell.ie>

Eircell, Ireland's largest mobile phone operator, presents new products, services and features on its fully-scalable Website On Eir. Interactive elements include; ONTRACK, a Fantasy Formula 1 game and Webtext, a Web-based text messaging service.

<www.whoseday.com>

The Whoseday Book brings together special contributions from 366 of Ireland's foremost writers, painters, poets, philosophers and personalities. The Website's development is sponsored by Webfactory who produced a fully secure solution to allow users to order the book online, the proceeds of which go to the Irish Hospice Foundation.

<www.readytogo.ie>

Hugo is familiar to most Irish people as the bright, bubbly front man of the Ready to Go brand. The Ready to Go Website took his character, and personality, and used the interactive capabilities of the Internet to allow users to really communicate with him, and consequently the Ready to Go brand. A Macromedia Shocked Site of the Day winner.

```
</frameset>
<noframes>
<br><br>
```

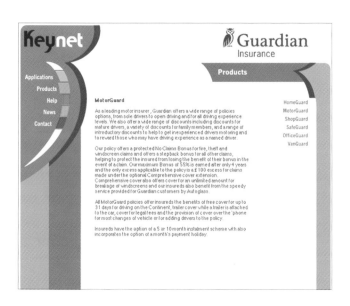

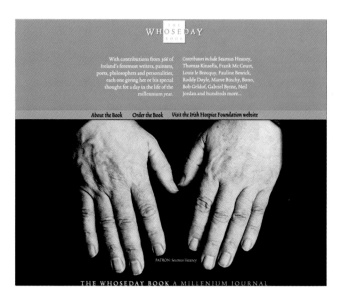

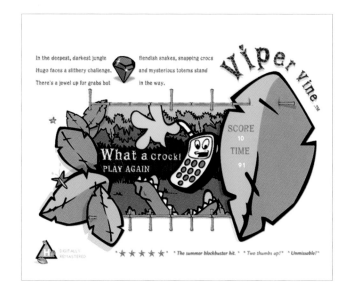

<index>
<one show interactive vol. II>

>

</pageref>
259><rhp>

</pageref>
<260><lhp>

\>

\

</pageref>
<263><rhp>

</pageref>
<264><lhp>

</pageref>
<265><rhp>

<multimedia>

</pageref>
<266><lhp>

>

</pageref>
<267><rhp>

>

</pageref>
<268><lhp>

</pageref>
<269><rhp>

</pageref>
<272><lhp>